MUSINGS OF A MILITARY MAVERICK

MUSINGS OF A MILITARY MAVERICK

Yoginder Sharma

PARTRIDGE

ISBN:	Hardcover	978-1-4828-7285-9
	Softcover	978-1-4828-7284-2
	eBook	978-1-4828-7283-5

To order additional copies of this book, contact
Partridge India
000 800 10062 62
orders.india@partridgepublishing.com

www.partridgepublishing.com/india

Acknowledgement

I owe this work to

THAT

Nameless, Formless and Infinite

Source of 'everything' including the

INSPIRATION

and Intuitive Ideas which make up this book;

It also manifested

In the form of love and support of my family

Despina, Athena and Arun;

and support of extended family, especially Komal, my niece

as also warm blessings of many friends like

Gracyma, Emma, Vidyulatha

I am grateful for the excellent staff support from

Navin Kumar Singhal, S Stalin, MRK Reddy

I thank the supporting members of Partridge Publications

Especially Jules, Farrina, Gemma and Pearl.

I wish to pay a special tribute to the great Indian
Army and the GRENADIERS.

(Note: THAT comes from *Vedantic* **'Tat Tvam Asi'**-Thou Art That)

Preface

TRIBUTE TO A SOULMATE- OCT 2013

A young Army officer from India and a Greek girl met in Gaza during 1958. They did not fall in love at first sight. It happened slowly as a subtle process of nature; real romances rarely run like movie scripts.

Both had roots in traditional families. They came from diverse cultural and civilisational backgrounds. Their polarised roots provided a touch of mystique to an extraordinary story- a voyage of togetherness of fifty-five years, through high tides, tsunamis, and smooth sailing. The robust tree that spawned from these roots stands as a testimony of blessedness of that meeting.

Despina 1957

This is a slice of their life. In fact, it is our story, which is also connected with half a century of my Regimental heritage.

It was the call of duty and destiny that brought us together. Both of us were serving with the United Nations Emergency Force (UNEF) at that time. UNEF was a multi-national force comprising of contingents from Brazil, Canada, Denmark, India, Norway, Sweden, Yugoslavia, and International civil staff. It was deployed in the Sinai Peninsula to keep peace between Egypt and Israel, consequent to the Arab Israeli war of 1956. The nationalisation of the Suez Canal in 1956 had led to the Anglo-french invasion of the Canal Zone and the Israeli blitz through the Sinai. The bombings and para-drops over Ismailia (HQ of the Suez Canal Company) had also hit the Greek quarter, and pounded some residential buildings, including one occupied by the Monioudis family.

The family patriarch, Pericles M., had migrated here as a young sailor in typical Hellenic seafaring tradition. He had come from the Aegean island of Chios, which is across the straits from the port town of Krini (now *Cesme*) on the Asia-Minor landmass. The family had owned agricultural assets there until driven out by the Ottoman Empire. Pericles drifted into the Suez Canal Zone and found his greener pastures as also his lady-love in the local Greek community. They raised a family of six that was heavily influenced by the mixed (Egyptian, Greek, French, and Italian) cultures of the town.

A premature heart attack in 1952 left his widow with four unsettled children. The elder daughters had been married off into the Greek diaspora in Cyprus and Australia. The burden of supporting the family thus came on the young shoulders of the next two siblings-namely, Andony and Despina - both in their early twenties. It was fortuitous that they found employment with the UNEF in 1956 based on their multilingual skills. During the next two years, the Israeli forces kept vacating the occupied areas in the Sinai, and the UNEF kept moving from the Canal Zone into the Gaza Strip.

In 1958, my Unit, Second Battalion the GRENADIERS - was selected for service with the UNEF. Our Rifle Coys were deployed to patrol the Armistice Demarcation line, while the HQ was located at Deir-el-Balah, a hamlet some 16 kms from Gaza. We had to frequently visit Gaza for official and social purposes. I had a special interest in the only available squash court located within the military governor's complex as squash was a competition sport of UNEF- I did win the silver medal in 1959!

The Indian Provost and Postal units were the natural staging posts for our visits. By a coincidence (or a designer-quirk of destiny), the UN Staff member attached to these Indian units was the Greek Girl from

Officers Mess Jan 1959

x

Ismailia, Despina! And that was where and how we met; the rest, as they say, is history.

The fast and furious minds amongst you may have conjured up imagery of boy meets girl--- hormones rage--- romance flames! Mercifully, not all stories follow such basic-instinct recipes of lust and sensuality. Real life is more sublime and for a good reason. In a multiple 'boy meet girl' scenario matching options are unlimited, and mutual compatibility is the key. In this case also there was no scarcity of suitors for this bubbly young lady; and the forbidding presence of the Big Brother was a firewall against 'loose cannon' advances!

Our initial encounters were not only awkward but predictably disastrous. By default, no two people could be more mismatched! She was a gregarious, fun loving 'people's person' who loved parties, music, dancing and fun-times. And I was a certified introvert- a champion loner and award winner in the 'socially handicapped' category; timid, tongue-tied and with two left feet! She was articulate (six languages), assertive, and a multi-tasker and loaded with confidence, class and a bigger pay cheque. I could barely manage to pay for the 'scotch guzzling style' of the Indian 'officers and gentlemen' of the time!

Despite various opportunities to socialise, our cold-start remained in deep- freeze for many a month. The advent of the festive season viz. Diwali, Christmas and the Republic Day celebrations in the Unit did help somewhat. These created space for mutual understanding of common values- personal and cultural. The wild revelry of the Indian festival of colours (Holi) enabled some emotional intimacy. In the process we discovered our common humanity, the universality of human relationships, as also an underlying Indo-Greek affinity. All these ran deeper than the differences of roots, region and religious dogma. Nature too has willed that 'opposites attract'- to complement the 'yin and yang' (*Shiva and Shakti*) within human nature.

During my earned leave in Europe in Apr-May 59 I sensed some emotional-pangs of separation. A picture post-card from Rome declaring '*Mi manchi molto, Despina*' (miss you very much, D) was the first recognition of stronger stirrings. Yet there was no thought of a deeper commitment- so scary were the cultural gaps.

Many months later, while she was vacationing in Cyprus, where her eldest sister lived, I hopped across from the UN Leave-Center in Beirut to take a car trip around that exotic Island. That provided us with a fresh opportunity to bridge any gaps. The interactions with the family in Nicosia (as also earlier in Ismailia during my visits to Cairo) expanded our common-spaces. We discovered that beneath the visible skin-skeletal-societal distinctions there is a common framework of human values. I found that Greek families loved, laughed, and indulged baser emotions just like us; and that all parochial pigeon-holes are man-made. All humans fall short of the 'ideal' and the infirmities of flesh and mind are personal, not culture-centered.

It was inevitable that a meeting of minds would evolve into a soul-connection, leading to a commitment. In our starry-eyed romantic state we were inclined to discount future problems! Soon it was Dec 59 and the Indian Contingent was embarking on its return voyage at Port Said. I was the Ship Adjutant and more than neck-deep in work. Despite that well-meaning friends like Satish Walia (later Col Walia) created opportunities for us to say our farewells. No one could have known that along with farewell, there would be a promise of 'Au Revoir-I shall be back'.

Even I had no clue about how or when? Perhaps, even Despina did not believe it seriously, considering it a 'pacifier to a crying baby'. In this day and age, esoteric thoughts like 'word of honour' are hardly common currency! But for a hard-core Indian Grinder, a promise was sacrosanct. In essence, it was a blind leap of faith between two trusting souls. The battles that ensued were fought on many fronts.

On the family front the Greek Orthodox mindset exploded first-over the heretic thought of marriage to an Indian. A friendship was fine but an alliance with a pagan from an alien planet was unthinkable, akin to hara-kiri! Closer to the nerve, the prospect of losing the pillar of family support rankled badly - the younger brother in Athens was still job-hunting after his University education. The stratagems of family resistance kept stiffening- but so did the resolve of our' Gritty Girl'. She declared that sacrifices for the family could not be limitless and she had full faith in her man- 'He will be back'- and, when he does return, the ultimatum read- 'Bless us joyfully or I shall go alone!' Remarkably, it had got ratcheted to this level with little help from me! I still consider this as the ultimate in implicit trust and inspired guts- a gift of true love!

In contrast, my family's response was more muted and manageable. I dropped the bomb-shell during a Thanksgiving visit with Dad to a temple in Delhi. He was cool-just checked out if it was a 'done deal' or a 'case under consideration'. On confirmation that it was the former, his response was remarkably phlegmatic- "It is a personal life-choice and you are grown up-hopefully capable of taking the right decisions." This exchange seems so untypical that a brief glimpse of my family background is in order.

Till the start of twentieth century, my forefathers were settled in Hazara district adjoining Afghanistan. The family's earning potential from land and logistic support to British Army's Anglo-Afghan wars was shrinking. That tempted some family elders to be lured by offers of free land in border areas of Muzaffarabad in Jammu &Kashmir (J&K) State. So like the Monioudis family, my folks too had migrated into greener pastures at about the same time.

It was here that an inventive mechanical *charkha (spinning wheel)* designed by my father as a school boy was exhibited before the visiting Maharaja (king) of J&K. He was so impressed with the gifted lad of his State that he sanctioned a scholarship for an engineering degree from the Banaras Hindu University, and, thereafter practical training in the United Kingdom. Consequently my father spent many years in the UK imbibing its liberal and enlightened values. Little wonder then that his response was so enabling and easy!

We were brought up in different faiths- Greek Orthodox and *Sanatana Dharma* (literally, the 'eternal faith'). This was expected to be our toughest challenge; but it was not! In our inner-most core, we both felt that the Infinite and Universal Creator was One- and that was the 'essence of faith', not the superficial diversities or dogmas! We believed that we could harmonize our faiths. Our life has been a testimony to that. As the good Book says 'three things last forever- faith, hope, and love; and the greatest is love'!

In early 1960, I applied for security clearance to marry a foreign national and the case was sent to Army Headquarters, duly recommended by my CO. In Feb, it came back for resubmission, as a new policy had come into force requiring a letter of resignation to be submitted along with the application. This was as recoil to a case wherein a Major denied permission had taken the case to a court of law on grounds of denial of a fundamental freedom! But who can 'deter the determined' in love and war?

A saving grace in the new Policy was the stipulation that a decision will be taken within six months. So in mid-Aug I chose to dare the system by flying back to Egypt and doing what had to be done, on assumption of 'deemed-sanction'! I had already put in my papers-so what could get worse?

Gen Burns - Bidding Farewell

We had a simple traditional ceremony to meet the bottom-line wish of her family, on 15 Aug. In Dec 60 when formal sanction was received, after due security clearances, we regularised the record, as per provisions of Indian Special Marriages Act 1955.

An interesting side-story is worth recounting. I came to know later that I seemed to have hurt the ego of my Commanding Officer (CO), by a tactless comment during a conference that he chose to endorse 'not recommended' on my second-time application for marriage. Fortunately, other commanders in the chain took a mature view that 'unless there is a security objection, the officer should be permitted to marry anyone of his choice'. It must have been a part of the higher design to enable two soul-mates to unite!

Meanwhile, the UN had become involved in peace-keeping operations in Congo and staff was being milked from existing Forces. Orders had been received for Despina's transfer to Congo- as if her present problems were not enough! To match my madness, she preferred to resign and jump blind into a hopeless void with me. That the gamble paid off and we overcame every challenge over the next 50 years is history now. To have risen from a maverick Captain's wife to be First Lady of an Army Command (next in protocol to Chief's wife) and be anointed the First Lady of The GRENADIERS is nothing short of a miracle.

Despina arrived in India and embraced my family with such endearing warmth and sincerity that it stunned the sceptics and silenced the cynics. When we went up to the family Patriarch and bowed down for his blessings, he asked *'Yeh Kaun?'* (Who is this?); about the girl in the western dress. *'Yogi ki Unani Bahu'* (Yogi's Greek bride) said my Dad. *'Unani, phir thik hai- hamare jaise log hain* (Greek; then it's OK, they are just like us'!) and patted our heads warmly. Such is the residual impact of past interactions between these two ancient civilisations.

First Couple of the Grenadiers

In her turn, Despina's impact on my family is poignantly reflected in the words of my youngest sibling (now a former Chief Engineer of J&K state) (who as a 10 yr old had sat in her lap as per Punjabi custom during the ceremonial-reception when I had first taken her home). It reads:-

'Today we lost our Dearest Bhabhi, Despina Sharma, wife of Gen Sharma. She came from Greece after marrying our brother in 1960 and became more Indian than us. She changed the quality of our lives and family relations with so much love and affection towards one and all. Want to write more but tears won't stop-what will my Brother do without her?'

What indeed? The rich blessings of our life together are another story. Maybe, for another day!

It was on 4 October 2013, that the 'Grand Weaver of Divine Designs' decided that our time together in this 'journey of souls' was over. It is not given to us humans to predict, prevent or interfere with the higher design. A lesson that I have learnt over a life-- time is that nothing happens by chance or coincidence or without a purpose.

In case the preceding account speaks anything to you, as it does to me, you may find some sense in my belief that, there will be an Au Revoir- a mad promise made to her again! Do keep your minds open for there is so much more between heaven and earth that is beyond human awareness!

She had wanted me to write this account since long, for posterity's sake-especially in this era of fractured families. I started a few weeks ago and read out substantial parts while she was still conscious. She approved and thanked me. I know it is heavy with contextual details, without which the 'flesh and blood' feel would be lacking. Am sharing it, for what it is worth, with family, friends and mainly the Grinder Family, which has been our '*dharma-kshetra (field of ethical action)* and *karma-bhoomi (field of duty)*' for much of our lives. It is not for me to speak of her contribution to the Regiment- others know it better. But I can vouch for her love and commitment to the GRENADIERS family-so deep, genuine and intense was it, that I could never match it. Let us celebrate that.

Prologue

My Tribute to a Soul-mate touched many a sentimental chord. It also challenged some conservative mind-sets. A few amongst them labeled us as mavericks for being unconventional, loose-cannons! Some smart-alecs (and cassandras) were curious about 'Who converted whom? I resisted a reflexive response so as not to trivialise the issue!

Final Resting Place - 2014

That was a small-slice of our life- a nostalgic recall of the start of a journey together. Small-bites are generally served as appetisers before the main meal! On impulse, I have chosen to add more slices to the story of that fateful encounter between two strangers. It may whet the appetite of the curious and de-mystify the maverick-mystique, somewhat. It is not a tale of heroics or humour; just the back-story of a fauji (military)-family!

The narrative of that Tribute had closed with the end of a Soul-mate's earthly journey. A year later as I look at the traditional marker of the site where her mortal remains rest- to be joined by my ashes at 'sunset'- the deluge of emotions has subsided but reflections run deeper.

I ponder over the significance of this black-white-grey structure. Is it a memorial or a metaphor? To me, it is a symbolic *sangam* of two waves that rose continents apart, converged to create their own ripples and rejoin Infinity from which they had risen! But is our existence just a 'dust unto dust' story; or does it transcend the physical-self? We need to seriously look back at our roots in search of our 'true- self'!

As I dig for roots I keep going deeper into the unending-unknown? This is so as eternity is the nature of existence. Is this then a search 'from Eternity to Here'! The defining logic is that if ever there was no 'existence' there would be nothing. Since nothing can come *from* nothing, it would mean non-existence ever-after!

Lest I get more abstract, I shall pre-empt the fog of philosophy with real-life! Whenever someone 'catty' asked Despina about my roots, she faced impossible options. Was I a Dogra from Jammu, my home-town; a Kashmiri-Punjabi from Muzaffarabad, which is my birthplace in Jammu & Kashmir; Or a Hazara Brahmin from AFPAK region or inheritor of some ancient gotra-lineage?

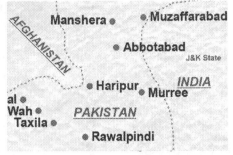

Happily for her I was just a mixed-up Indian OG-Fauji (Military Olive Green) of the GRENADIERS family; married to a *foreigner* who was innocent about such cultural-compartments. In-service, our caste was military-gypsies and in matters of faith we were fully soaked in the secular-ethos of soldiering!

Her tongue-in-cheek response used to be-'Ask him! I bet he does not know. By the way, why have you left out the Aryan migrations or Alexander's legacy; and does all this really matter to anyone?' Indeed, does one's origin or identity really matter these days? That is a moot question; but rootlessness is the primary cause of pervasive selfishness; and narrow Identity-politics, which is the most ominous threat of our times!

My exploration of 'roots' led me into esoteric domains. These included archeo-genetics (flow of DNA groups since 200,000 BCE), my genetic lineage (Paternal genetic-group Q and Maternal Haplogroup U2- originating 20 to 35000 years ago); as also relevant aspects of civilisational, cultural and caste identities! These are dense and deep areas, mysteriously intertwined with our 'presents'- and they are heavy stuff!

I have chosen not to bludgeon you with these now, may be later! I shall therefore cut to the quick- to the less complex, lighter and more readable parts of my story, as it evolved in real life.

CHAPTER 1

From Cradle To Commissioning

It was a special day at the engineer's residence, in the premises of the power house. A son—the firstborn of the first-wife of the power *parivar (family)*—was born. Few newborns can hope for a better beginning; a celebrity father (publicly anointed as the Sun of Muzaffarabad, for electrifying the town), two doting Mothers (real-sisters) and a silver bowl (*katora),* instead of a spoon. That *katora* became a trademark- the sky would fall if it went missing as, *Raja-beta* (the prince) would not drink milk without it.

The *rasoi-report* (staff gossip) about the new 'bundle in the cradle' was that it had an oversized head and short legs. The former was celebrated as a cerebral future but the latter disturbed the engineer-father. He kept checking, with a slide-rule, whether the design defect was a disability or deformity. No one suspected then, or later, that this Infant would grow up to be an Infantryman, a Ranger-Commando and a General (with a game-leg)! Does our beginning ever reflect the end? Hardly! It is all in the DNA and destiny, both of which are unpredictable and beyond our control.

But genes don't lie! If so, a reality-check of the preceding generations would serve a purpose here. My freshly famous father was from an average agricultural family. The forefathers had owned land in the hills near Mansehra in Hazara District of erstwhile North West Frontier Province (NWFP) bordering Afghanistan. The family supplemented its income by arranging logistic-support for British forces fighting in Afghanistan. While doing so the men-folk would often accompany the army columns. Survival in a harsh and hostile environment was thus their staple, and it paid-off at the time of the blood-soaked partition of India in 1947.

Our mothers' were raised in a conservative family of Haripur. They were steeped in tradition and essentially equipped to run a home and bring up families- hence literates in own-language only. All the education and enculturation was done at home, in the absence of schools for girls. The outside world was not an equal-opportunity environment for girls but at home *shakti* (female-power) was the ruling deity. And women guarded that space jealously even aggressively, despite the feudal-paternal frontier-Punjabi culture. The social-milieu of the time may seem irrelevant today but it has lessons for us about clarity of roles and management of space in relationships.

Our only grandparent who overlapped with us was the charismatic *Nana-ji* (mother's father). He was a 'gentleman of class'—English-educated at Abbotabad (lately of Osama fame); a war veteran, who later joined forest service on demobilisation. He was indeed a colourful figure- a certified scout-master, a freedom-fighter, an amateur Ayurveda healer and a follower of Arya Samaj (a reformist Hindu movement). His children from the third wife in his 70s, are younger to me in age. At six-foot plus, he was a formidable figure, be it in western clothing or as a gun-toting Pathan in Frontier style. He felt fully fulfilled when my son was commissioned as an officer. Coincidentally, *Nana ji* was cremated the day after- Despina and I had gone with celebratory sweets when he was being wheeled out for his last ride.

I faintly recall our Nani. She did not keep good health and passed away in my infancy. I learnt later that as treatment for chronic pain the local quack had got her addicted to an opiate-drug, a pet produce of Afghanistan. The habit became irresistible and she became a prescription-addict. It is hard to tell whether it was this, or the *soma*-guzzling tradition of our ancient progenitors, that was the origin for the family fondness for overindulgence. But it must be a genetic-mutation as it went beyond my maternal lineage. More than a few siblings, cousins and nephews have seriously succumbed to temptations of bottled *'spirits'!*

A flashback to our roots is relevant here. How did we get to be in this remote tribal corner of North-West India? Hazara Region had been at crossroads and a stamping ground of many powers and people- the Bactrian-Greeks, Mauryans, Kushans, Afghans, Turks, British and the Sikhs, as also migrants from neighbouring areas viz Kashmir and the Punjab. They have all walked this land since the pre—Vedic Indus-Saraswati Civilisation (pre 5000 BCE). Our roots were thus in an ethnic-remix of ancient Indus-Saraswati tribal people and migrants who came through the ancient 'silk—route'/Hindu-Kush passes. An overlay was added over that ancient extraction by later Hindu-Sikh migrants who came from the Punjab and Jammu areas in the wake of Maharaja Ranjit Singh's grand army which captured all of North West India, including Afghanistan and parts of Kashmir(up to Tibet-border). It is not possible that there was an ethnic-vacuum in Hazara before Ranjit's Singh's campaign or the Islamic invasions of 8th century CE- hence the first part of my proposition about our ancient roots!

Let me get back to recent times. It was the lure of land that had tempted my father's elder brothers to migrate from their homeland in Hazara to Muzaffarabad into the contiguous J&K State, around the turn of 20th century. Our grandparents had already passed-on. Two brothers staked claim on the land on either bank of Kishanganga River, downstream of

S Ujagar Singh flanked by his Son, Me and Madan (my youngest brother)

its junction with River Jhelum. Muzaffarabad is a picturesque Shangri-la like valley nestling between the hills and the river junction, at Domel. Since rivers have only two banks for staking a claim, the youngest sibling was packed off to Srinagar for studies. The rest, as they say, is history.

I have already shared the story of recognition of my father's technical-talent and royal-sponsorship to study Engineering at Banaras Hindu University (BHU), and the UK. While abroad, he was mindful of the socio-economic realities at home and resisted all distractions. He focused on gaining practical experience and in the process imbibed the spirit of

English enterprise and work ethic. He came back safe and single despite temptations. And a search for a suitable-match was launched by well wishers

But an insidious maverick streak prevailed and he preferred a challenge to a secure career and family life. He felt that his qualifying as an electrical engineer was futile if his hometown remained in the dark. So he chose to electrify it through self-help and private-enterprise. He was supported by a team of spirited *Sardars*, who were initially hired as personal staff, but later became lifelong family friends. The last one of that vintage, Sardar Ujagar Singh, died recently at 105, a few months after I met him in Jammu in 2014.

That intrepid team of pioneers cut the hillside to channel water, erected imported turbines and generators (bought with money raised as loans from the locals), and commissioned the power supply, all on their own in early 1930s. It was an incredible turnkey job, all planned and executed by a young engineer and his band of karmic brothers.

The power house in Muzaffarabad drew immense attention towards my father. The Maharajas of J&K and Jodhpur had inaugurated it. Such high-profile recognition became irksome into some ego-driven segments and triggered a demand for early refund of loans taken to finance the project. The upshot was that he had to sell his Power- house to the government (except the house where I was born). Sadly that too was lost to Pakistani raiders when they invaded Kashmir in October 1947.

My father was absorbed, as the second Indian engineer, in State government service. Thereafter he moved on to other professional

Dad with Me (in front), the Turbine and Baldev (Mums' brother) in 1945. This first ever Indian designed Turbine was later installed as a hydro-power project in UP State in 1951. This was our second private power house.

achievements; but the earlier creative detour cost him the Chief Engineer's job. He was beyond caring for power, position or possessions as long as he could follow his passion. His values of 'Work is worship' and selfless 'professional commitment' are the greatest gifts and blessings passed on to us. But there was a flipside to that single minded work-ethic, as would be seen later.

Meanwhile, family pressure to settle down had kept mounting. So he took a break from work to select a bride from a short-list of suitable girls from Hazara *Biradari (fraternity)*. With two grown-up girls, our Nana's home was a natural pitstop. A direct boy-meet-girl encounter was unthinkable those days. An indirect peek through a door into the '*zenana*' (ladies section) was all that was socially acceptable. Perhaps, he was thinking of a water-turbine (or some old flame in London) as he nodded approval to a vague target-indication towards the elder daughter, who was surrounded by a brood of girls. His implied approval sent a cheer of celebration and negotiations started for settling the wedding date.

At the time of reception of the *Baraat (marriage party),* the groom discovered that the bubbly-girl of his choice was the younger-sister, not the plain-Jane proposed bride. Malicious minds muttered '*dhoka (deception)*' but the sensible elders understood that the problem had been created by a visual-parallax error. In the explosive frontier culture such a mix-up was sufficient cause for loaded guns to come into action. *Gussa (rage)* sits very lightly on the *high-noses* of Frontiersmen. The family elders found a creative solution. They proposed that he marries both sisters. It may seem weird and unfair by modern sensibilities but at the time it was acceptable to all, except perhaps the traumatised bride-to-be. But she had no voice and a lot of common-sense. Plural marriages were a norm amongst higher social classes of the time. In fact, for aristocracy it symbolised a higher status.

It was thus that the seven of us (five sons from the elder wife and a daughter and son from the younger) came to have twin mothers. We called them *Badi* and *Choti* Ma-jee (elder and younger moms) respectively. Others may have had a problem juggling labels of mothers, *masis* (aunts) or step-mothers, but none of that bothered us. We were one big happy family, except when feuding over cream or crumbs!

Many years later, my newly-wed wife, Despina was shocked by this strange family setting. But it was working so well that a double mother-in-law became a welcome prospect. In case of an emotional bump with one, a handy back-up was readily available. Indeed, it was not always a 'sugar and honey' scenario; but if you can show me a family which is free of ego-bumps I will show you a liar's den! A unique feature in this case was the sisterly dimension, which enabled easy resolution of ego clashes and trivial differences. The common bloodline (*maika*) was a cushion. We have witnessed the finest face of this uncommon family setting, but would not recommend it for general adoption. Sadly, one does detect dissonance in relations within the third generation, mainly due to ignorance or perceived inheritance imbalances!

Is this a sanitised picture of my childhood? Maybe it is, if viewed from a cynic's perspective. By its nature, real life is made up of many shades of grey and pairs-of-opposites! There is no sunshine without a shadow or angels without feet-of-clay- or hardly ever? My childhood was no exception. But I shall have to dig very deep to recall all black or dark-grays of my early life. It has become a fetish to blame childhood influences or incidents to rationalise one's personal weaknesses and flaws; as if anyone was promised a perfect personality or destiny. Indeed, my parents were not perfect and siblings a bunch of buffoons, servants were scoundrels and neighbours a nuisance. Yet my childhood remains a mix of warm, beautiful and bitter-sweet memories. Was I specially blessed or is this just make-believe? All reality is, in fact, a make-belief of our perceptions!

It would diminish me in my own eyes to attribute my inabilities to rough realities of childhood. Indeed, my work-obsessed father was less inclined and found lesser time to tend to us (so he provided two mothers to compensate). He had a short fuse and a lethal look that could set off shivers or wet-streams; and the tiger-moms were menacing in their *Kali* (angry Goddess) avatar. They did not pamper brattiness and believed in giving us a Spartan upbringing, in ancient *Gurukul* (ashram) tradition.

But there were no flesh and blood 'gurus' for me due to remote locations of my father's postings. Generally, hydel-power plants/ projects are located in way-out places in the wilderness.

Consequently, I was privately tutored for many years, by under-qualified primary school teachers from nearby villages. Can I blame anybody for such deprivations? In the real world no one gets a choice of parentage, places or privileges. We were taught to be happy in whatever was and learnt to count our blessings. The deprived socialisation in my formative years had a silver lining- there was no tension due to competition or contact of any undesirable kind. But it did prove to be a severe handicap in later life, particularly in the military academy!

This has been a rambling recall of my reflections so far- let me get a bit organised now. The decade of 1937-47 was hectic at many levels. Due to periodic transfers of my Father we had to move from Muzaffarabad to Baramulla, Jammu, Mahora (near Uri), outskirts of Srinagar and back to Jammu. Meanwhile the family had kept adding a new member every two years or so to reach a healthy score of six brothers and one sister- both Mothers were fully engaged in multiplying the family and running the growing home establishment. It invariably included a couple of cows (and other pets), a typical *tandur* for making 'makki ki roti' (corn bread). We lived in huge bungalows with acres of gardens, fruit trees and a horde of servants.

The family drove in Dad's English car (one of a dozen in the State), through verdant valleys and vast forests to go from one place to another. There was no railway or air network existing then. All that is the stuff of dreams now! It was an idyllic and a privileged life in the salubrious setting of '*firdaus bar ru-e zamin*' (heaven on earth) as Kashmir was known to be since Mughal times. And then, all that peace and calm was shattered by the boom of guns and a shooting war.

In Aug 1947, two years after the end of World War II, an exhausted British Raj abruptly granted Independence to India and fractured it into two. Kashmir became a political victim of aggression and the wounded valley has been bleeding ever since. In the competing power grab for indecisive princely states that dithered about merger with India or Pakistan, Pak-sponsored tribals invaded Kashmir in October 1947. These raiders (hordes of tribals armed, abetted and led by Pakistani military) overcame the overstretched State forces and marauded their way up to the doorstep of Srinagar. Both sides of our family lost their homes and property and were stranded, rendered refugees, captured and worse- one in Pakistan (NWFP) and the other in Occupied Kashmir.

At the time, my father was a Divisional engineer in-charge of a project in an outlying district but the family was staying in Srinagar. The only lifeline of Kashmir valley which ran through Muzaffarabad-Uri-Baramulla-Srinagar has remained cut-off since then. The isolation so imposed resulted in essential supplies and survival needs getting exhausted. A strict rationing system was enforced, including on fuels, salt, sugar, medicines etc. There was no power supply as Mahora Power House (our happy-home of many years) had been over-run. Incidentally, my cousin RL Sharma (who had followed my father to BHU) was the Engineer in-charge. He had to take shelter with the Army, after its loss and subsequent re-capture. Later my father was co-opted for expert assistance during rehabilitation of the plant -such was the recognition of his technical genius! He received an effusive letter of commendation for this contribution from the Chief Engineer, on behalf of the Government.

We were witnesses to the shooting war raging at the doorstep of Srinagar, not far from our residence. From the rooftop I could see our aircraft strafing enemy positions during the crucial battle of Sheltang. Sheikh Abdullah, the National Conference leader mobilised public support against PAK- raiders and appealed for SOS help to India. I also marched with student processions.

Meanwhile the fate of our families in Pakistan and POK (Pakistan Occupied Kashmir) was unknown, except for disturbing leaks from across the border. Only after the formal accession of the State with the Indian Union and the lightning- speed airlift of Indian Army units into Srinagar (hours before airport's impending loss) did the tide begin to turn. Thus began the baptism by fire of new India's Armed forces- a long saga of sacrifice, success and valour. But the roll back was prematurely ended in the vain hope that the United Nations intervention will bring about a just and honourable peace. Instead of that it created a 'No War-No Peace' stalemate that continues to date. It is now one of the worst conflict-flashpoints in the world. But that is another story-I would rather revert to my own.

In late 1948, my father was transferred to Jammu to take charge of a new division responsible for creating a water-supply system for all of Jammu province. There was no way for us to move as Army convoys had choked the road space. Finally, the government arranged for us to be lifted in two 3-ton vehicles as a part of the down convoy. This was the family's first ride in Army transport- an experience that has stretched to include two generations and hopefully will last longer.

In Jammu we got a hired house to live in, which was barely adequate for a small family. Meanwhile news arrived that survivors of families on the other side of the Border were being evacuated under the aegis of Red Cross, to refugee camps being set up in Punjab, UP and Delhi. It took months of searches to trace them amongst tens of thousands that were pouring in daily from across the blood-soaked borders.

The maternal side of my family was collected by my Nana ji and re-settled in evacuated homes in Najafgarh, near Delhi. His only son Baldev had stayed on with his sisters, since our Nani's death in early '40s. He was like an elder sibling to me. Sadly he died prematurely in 1951, in his sister's arms, due to a congenital heart condition.

My father took charge of the family of his middle brother who had been killed by the raiders. RL did the same for his parents and siblings. Our combined joint family strength was now over 16. All of us were sheltered, raised, educated and settled by my father. Our cramped living conditions resembled life as on a railway platform. But it had all the warmth of a home. We learnt to share and co-exist in the available space, cheerfully and peacefully. Our elders taught us, by example, that 'you don't need a huge house or high means but a big heart to live in harmony'!

My formal schooling started in these trying times. I was admitted into a good Government school-Sri Ranbir High School, Jammu- a few months before the final examination of 8th class. To add to my misery I came down with typhoid and was still recovering at exam-time. Despite medical advice to the contrary, a stubborn streak said 'Go on and get it over with!' I fluked a pass and was surprised to get a school scholarship for top score in science. Friends insisted that I treat them to a movie, and I did. When I got home, my mother said 'go offer your first earning to your father and seek his blessings'. I sheepishly confessed that I had spent it all on friends; she admonished but gave me money, which Dad doubled and gave back. This was the first exposure of my naiveté in matters of sensitivity and propriety; a lesson that I am still to learn fully.

It was taken for granted that I shall follow the family career line of engineers, which dictated options of subjects and stream of study. In 1949, my School started an experiment of a special section for gifted students, under a selected form- master, Shri Tej Ram Khajuria. He was a martinet but a *Guru* in the finest tradition of the term. And I was one of his favourites. Many years later, when serious riots had broken out in Jammu, curfew was imposed and Army deployed, I as the Chief of Staff of the Corps went to *Masterji's* home with the Officer-In-Charge and directed that he be taken care of as befitting my Guru. They did and he was touched; but it was so small a gesture of gratitude for his immeasurable gifts to us! Till the end of his life, in his 80s, he used to walk up to *Vaishno Devi* Shrine, as he had done every month of his disciplined life. By example, he had taught us the value of 'selfless-service as a gift of giving' with no concern for rewards.

Kashmir University became functional in 1950 and imposed an age bar of 14 years for School finals (10th). I was underage because of a couple of double-promotions in early years. All sane counsel said 'repeat the year and you will excel next time.' My father knew me better and was sceptical. His view was that a repetition will bore and demotivate me and I shall fare worse. My school had high hopes in my getting a competitive position in the University, so they sided with my father. My view was, of course, irrelevant.

In fact my thinking was quite ambivalent- to me it was 'much ado about nothing'. I was sent to the education minister, who knew my Father, for seeking a special dispensation despite being underage. He listened patiently and advised, 'Son, go tell your headmaster to rectify your date of birth." And thus my age was stretched, with help from a pliant priest- there were no official birth certificates then. I did not disappoint the 'punters' and topped in Jammu province but was ranked 10th overall- it is not easy to beat the cerebral Kashmiri Pandits. It hardly mattered to me as I am anything but competitive.

With Dad and my brothers in 1972

At the end of my first year in the College, there was a special convocation. I was a surprise recipient of book-awards from the then PM of J&K State, for highest marks in two subjects! If, by now, you are exasperated by this one-sided portrayal of my brilliance, I empathise with you. It is a deceptive and skewed part-profile! The other part consists of an introverted, under-confident, awkward teen-ager, with an out-of-proportion body and challenged motor-skills; the chubby-cheeks concealed a sickly kid (annual malaria attacks, typhoid and tonsils) and an angst-ridden psyche. But why so- It makes no sense? How can anyone so privileged and having such an enviable performance profile be so mixed up? That is a fair question screaming for a response.

Here are my self-reflections – a tenuous exercise in pop-psychology yet good science. We exist as bubbles/waves in an ocean of a networked energy- field. Science tells us that our bodies consist of trillions of vibrating and intelligent cells, in the energy-field- remember we started with two! The sensors of these cells are constantly absorbing signals from the environment and responding as programmed.

Let me relate this to my own environment. The six of us are from the same gene pool and were raised almost identically. Yet our life-trajectories have been so different. It seems that each one's sensors picked up different signals i.e. more positive or negative energy than the others.

What about me- here are some wild guesses:-

- Despite her exalted status, the implicit rejection in the beginning had left an impact on my Mother's energy vibes. Those, in turn, added a degree of broodiness to my nature; but also her bulldoggish resilience.

- My own conflicted mental and physical abilities would have added a couple of complexes.

Baby of the Course-4ft11.93lbs-1st term

But these are my musings, not a psycho-analysis! I have merely mentioned these to indicate that our strengths and dichotomies are a part of our Being- accept life as it is and make the most of it! Our past may not be in our hands but OUR FUTURE IS.

My diffident nature had my father concerned. One day he came across a notification of entrance exam for the National Defence Academy. He saw it as a confidence-booster opportunity for my dormant potential - a sort of wake-up for the sleeping giant within. I am still searching for it! It was the last date of application. I was summoned to the Principal's office, and made to sign some forms, in a state of blissful cluelessness. The prospect of travelling to Delhi by train was sufficient motivation for me to fall in line.

By the evening my Dad had second thoughts- what about his dream of seeing me as an engineer! His confidant and nephew, RL, came to the rescue- he clarified that the Army also has engineers. He knew because his wife's seven brothers were in the Army (Dubey family), mostly engineers and many generals.

How did I negotiate the written examination and a five-day SSB Interview is a miracle beyond logic. The rigorous interview involved full time observation and assessment by a professional psychologist, a group-testing-officer and a qualified interviewing officer. I zombie-walked through all the tests. It was a touching display of innocence, complete lack of preparation, but supreme spontaneity. In fact, I was so honest as to tell them that my age was fudged and that I had little motivation for military service. I never got beyond the second obstacle out of ten, where each fetched points as per its serial number- simply because I could not catch the hanging tyre. I was 4 ft 11 in tall and weighed 91 lbs. I had needed a medical certificate to be admitted for tests, to the effect that I should reach the cut-off height of 5.2 ft, by grace of God and my genes.

By May 1951, at barely 15, I was a cadet in the Joint Services Wing of National Defence Academy at Dehra Dun, for a four-year long course to become an officer of the Indian Army. It was like an innocent boy being fed as raw material into the sausage-machine loftily called a Military Academy- now that is a bit melodramatic just for effect! Actually I was so naïve and free of fear that the next four years just passed as a forgettable phase of life. But they were the foundation of a richly rewarding career that has proved to be a lifetime passion.

This is getting schizophrenic- a split personality all over again. To understand, you will have to empathise with my state then. Fancy yourself as a sickly underdog, schooled in the back-of-beyond, thrown into the gladiators ring with burly bullies from the best public schools (including semi-Military schools). How would you react? Others in the same boat quit and ran but I seemed to have a survivor's spine, a bulldoggish streak.

I had been told that military training was specially designed to defreeze one to weed out the civilian and transplant a military persona and then reconstruct as a soldier. Some heavy-duty shock treatment and deprivation of socio-emotional support is on purpose and by design. So my response was- OK, go on do your worst- I shall cope. I may have been a midget in brawn-power and a total zero in social and sporting skills but never a quitter.

I realised that my competing on equal footing was a no-brainer. So I instinctively adopted a survival-mode and focussed on those domains where I had a chance. My legs were short but my lung-power was strong having been raised in the mountains. I had better endurance and could run longer. In the boxing ring I could be pluckier than my size opposition.

In management jargon this may be called SWOT analysis- but in my case it was the little man's survival instinct. And thus, for the next four years I kept my head above the water, survived and was commissioned. Being seriously competitive was not in my nature, nor reach or a goal. I managed to graduate in the middle of the batch, in the order of merit ranking. By the end of the career I had clawed my way to be amongst the top three, at C in C level of Army's command! But that journey had started very modestly, indeed.

On Commissioning -1955

Military rations and rigorous exercise had ensured that I rose to 5 ft 10 inch height and scaled a robust 150 lbs. The President of India was pleased to grant me a lifetime Commission as an officer of the Indian Army. My father proudly attended my Passing–out Parade in June 1955. He was happy that I had gained confidence- but was perplexed that I had not joined a technical branch and chosen a British Infantry Regiment viz. the GRENADIERS! He was disturbed at my frequent use of slang (swear-words) that he associated, from his days in London, with cockney-class. All in all, he was a proud and happy father. My mothers were ecstatic and my handsome younger brother was so jealous as to demand immediate admission into Military or Police Academy on the strength of the father's influence. Didn't I say that every pup in the pack is different!

I shall not cover training-trivia or any colourful anecdotes of personalities or events of my Academy days. However, you may get a flavour from the following- 'Shadows at Sunset' -based on my 2005 recall of those days, when we celebrated the Golden Jubilee of our commissioning.

"SHADOWS AT SUNSET

This account is based on a random recall of events related to the National Defence Academy of early 50's. Memories are like shadows, ephemeral and elusive. In the afterglow of a golden 'sunset', these are bound to be a mix of vague and woolly nostalgia.

It started with the first fall-in. A booming command from the high 'Tallest on the right and shortest......' resulted in a scramble. Everyone was sizing down the other, till humbled by reality-check! For a few at the high end it was a no-brainer. The 6ft tall Sikh (Mohinder Bal) was briefly eyeballed by a beefy batch-mate (DD Madura), but the turban ruled the right marker. At the other end there was no contest- amongst the undersized 5foot nothings- the 'ultimate underdog' sorted himself out. Later when the top-dogs became cadet capts/ under-officers, he held up his end, in true tradition of the 'boy on the burning deck'!

Being last in the line for years would give anyone a complex. He too nursed raw sensitivity. But the compensation was worth it- being left out of anything seriously competitive i.e. selections based on brawn or bravado. His revenge was when others sweated, he 'shammed' shamelessly- that is Survivors trick No 1, which hasn't failed him since. At worst, his tribe had to keep shouting 'buck up-buck up Dog (later Fox) Sqn' from the sidelines or senselessly clap at cricket matches, the favourite Sunday pastime of the then Comdt, Gen Habibullah.

The caste-structure within the corps of cadets is a reflection of the outside reality. The reasons are multi-dimensional- segmented along lines of old-school ties, entry-stream, region, and language or whatever-else. However, within a few months of the grinding-regime, most such distinctions got steam-rolled into military ethos. Many a new veneer was added, such as speaking english better than the English or Hindi like FM Cariappa, the then C in C. It is to the credit of the brilliant band of Instructors that a functional level of military leadership gets ingrained into all-comers.

The Adjutants of the times (Kit Kataria/Whig/Rajendra Singh), were awesome figures. They were the only ones to whom the Drill RSMs (Ayling/Pearce etc) deferred politely, the rest were barked at. The Indian Drill Staff, like Sub Maj Abdul Khader, also filled the role superbly, even without the 'swearing' skills of the former.

Almost twenty years later one of those Adjts (by then a Brig) and I were in the 1971 War, in the same sector. He blew up on a mine on 7/8 Dec and I a week later. At the limb-fitting centre in Pune, months later, he used to encourage the amputees to march like soldiers on their new limbs. 'Look at the *mast chaal* (military gait) of the CO Sahib' he would say. 'Sir, you laid the foundation, by failing me twice in the Drill Square test' was my prompt response. Not his fault really- no two limbs of mine worked in harmony in 1951!

Ultimately, it is the end product - the finest of young Military Leadership- crossing the Final Step into the Chetwode Building that is the most endearing and enduring memory of one's military life.

The NDA (JSW of our times) and the IMA are the finest, 'equal opportunity' launch-pads of military leadership. Nothing in life is 'equal for all' – nothing is equal about the 'order of merit', the Medals or the Sword of Honour? But we were all equipped with abilities and values that enabled each one to select one's own 'trajectory and target' in life and often achieve it 'against all odds'.

Many of our Mates have crossed- over- RIP to all; to those in the queue-Om Shanti!"

CHAPTER 2

Commissioning And Early Regimental Experience

In the military, commissioning is a rite of passage from a Gentleman Cadet to an Officer and a gentleman. In real terms, it is a lone star on the shoulder and extra exercise for the saluting arm! I was commissioned as an officer of the Indian Army on 2 June 1955.

Most Young Officers (YOs) acquire inflated egos and hyperactive-hormones. The latter were already raging and instigating all manner of basic-instinct behavior! For an adolescent all bounds exist to be broken. Much ink is spilt on tales of teen age (mis) adventures. In my book, anyone who has not explored natural impulses is a saint or a retard! I was neither, but only braggarts need to brag! The extra-star acts as an aphrodisiac and causes crushes and an erotic-pull towards petticoats, even on a washing line!

After commissioning, my friends and I went to Kashmir on a voyeuristic trip. It was peak tourist-time in the Valley. In the picturesque Moghal garden skirting the Dal Lake, we spied a senior from the Academy swaggering with a girl on his arm. He was a former Service cadet (from the ranks); they are treated as love gurus by the NDA types!

Our hero decided to find a soothsayer to predict his love life, and we followed! The con-man fed each one his ego pill till my turn came. He took one look and predicted 'someday you may also find a girl-friend; take help from family!' After this snooty-snub, I chose to focus on matters military only!

In July 1955, the two of us (Mehar and I) who had both been commissioned into The GRENADIERS reported for duty at the

Regimental Centre (GRC) at Nasirabad. The Centre primarily serves to train recruits for the Regiment. It is also the repository and fountainhead of Regimental traditions and legacy. A fifteen day orientation capsule was a logical stopover, enroute to our Units in the field, to enable us to learn the ethos of the Regiment.

But it turned out to be the silly season for stuffing us with reams of Regimental history and intimate details of silver trophies. We were fed an overdose of old battles as if to prepare us for the past wars!

A significant memory of our stay at the Centre was the formal dining-in ceremony. Maj. Charles Pawar, the officiating Commandant presided. His reputation as an authority on mess etiquette was legendary. Coming from an aristocratic lineage he was a stickler for class and customs. We had been briefed by all members of the Mess committee, the Pipe Major and even the wine-waiter, about the nuances of etiquette especially drinking of 'toasts'! There was no scope for a faux pas as none would escape the hawk's eye.

Maj Pawar's parent Unit was the Second to None-a title bestowed on our Battalion by the Prince of Wales (we were then the 'Prince of Wales Own, later King Edward VII's Own'. I was joining this Battalion, which made me the exclusive focus of hospitality, at the expense of Mehar, who felt easy about it! After a fill of the finest scotch, there were multiple toasts of sherry and port at dinner time. By the time the Pipers came in, my head was reeling.

The Chief host was in full flow during the post-dinner welcome speech, with copious recharges of cognac and a Cuban cigar! In my euphoric state, I also responded to his speech with equal eloquence (and incoherence)! But I barely managed to survive the dinner- somehow crawled back to the BOQ (bachelor officer quarter) and threw-up all five courses of dinner and the exotic liquors!

When I recovered the next evening, I was stunned by the applause for my confidence level, drinking capacity, and public-speaking skill. Even Capt. Oscar Thomas (later Col), one of the hard core professionals at the Centre, complimented and asked about the elocution training at the Academy!

That was our initiation into the Grinder family! In the process, I learnt a lesson on how to overcome low confidence and be super eloquent via an overdose of alcohol. I employed this trick right through my days of Regimental soldiering. But such alcoholic inoculation is also the road to ruination and has ended many a promising career, including the venerable Charles, who fought his last battle in a hospital bed in INS Ashwini, trying to look gallant in a Grinder tie!

This incident also reflects the contrast between the sophisticated drinking style then and the binge-drinking seen later. Both have harmful results, but the former certainly behoves officers and gentlemen!

At the time the Centre's living infrastructure was primitive. We lived in ramshackle World War II barracks surrounded by a sea of sand. There were barely enough trees to serve as squad posts for recruits training. It was not uncommon for deadly desert snakes to crawl into our bathrooms in search of cool corners despite no running water and dry sanitation (snakes have no ears nor smell sense). One learnt more survival techniques at that time than during my commando training later. In short, creature comforts were an unknown concept then!

The team at the Centre was highly spirited and experienced. Most officers were wartime non-regulars - EC, SS, or TC, all types of temporary commissions. As YOs we ranked as cattle class, only fit for PT, route marches, night duties, etc. The ruling mantra was that YOs must be seen not heard! It was not uncommon to hear 'Carry On, Subedar Sahib' and 'let us go to the Mess for gin and tonic' after mid-day. No wonder stress was an unknown problem then!

There was vigour and vitality of spirit, *josh,* amongst the ranks. The credit for that was owed to a hard core of robust and proud Junior Commissioned Officers (JCOs)and NCOs class, who were all battle hardened. And they jealously guarded their turf against all comers, especially the subalterns (YOs). Yet the Officers were respected and followed. We learnt that leadership has more to do with qualities of heart and human-touch rather than head and hard work only.

Soon I was on my way to join the Battalion, which was operationally deployed in my home State. From the transit Camp at Pathankot, it took three days in a 3-ton vehicle (seated on own trunk with bedroll as backrest) to reach the Unit. Due to unpredictable nature of the transit chain my ETA (estimated time of arrival) was flexible. One was on duty from the railhead, so what was the rush?

It was a coincidence that I met the 2IC of the Battalion in the Transit Camp mess. That did deprive me of some *french leave* in the City that I knew well. Due to tight convoy timings our departure next morning was before morning teatime. The thoughtful 2IC ordered a tea break at the first available watering hole. It was the most expensive Tourist cafe downtown. A plate full of exotic pastries and puffs was served. While making conversation to know the new YO, he elegantly nibbled at one while I polished off all the rest. He probably put me on the negative list as a guest and branded me a threat to 'food security' in the mess!

My Unit was holding the forward-most posts in the URI sector, facing Pakistani positions. The Rifle Coys were deployed on picquets ranging from 8,000 to 11,000 feet, all along the cease-fire line (now Line of Control –LoC). The Battalion base was located on the Uri plateau. The road to Muzaffarabad, my birthplace, and the Jhelum River ran through our base.

Every thing was dug down with overhead protection and much of our existence was underground. We lived in fighting-cum-living bunkers, which were gems of tactical architecture. I shared one with Capt (later Brig) Raza. It had a low entrance (on the leeward side of possible shelling) with an improvised 'loo' at the entrance. A front-end location enabled easy clearance of waste by the *Safaiwalas,* the sanitation staff. The improvisation of 'thrones' in those days was nothing but wooden crates (having top hole with collection pans attached), aptly called thunder boxes.

The adjacent entrance had 6 to 8 steps leading to a sandbagged living space. It had two mud bunks with a dug-out channel in between, for sit-down work. Shelves and niches were carved into mud walls as a touch of class! Thick logs and heavy mud provided overhead protection and side apertures were provided for ventilation and use of weapons.

It was exotic but it did become a bit claustrophobic at times. It was some relief that the mess and a few office structures were over-ground. The officers team was an assorted group spanning a wide spectrum of professionalism (see photograph for a sample). Our Old Man, the CO, was the nearest thing to a silent and unsmiling *Buddha*. He had already commanded a Camel battalion and believed that '*hukam*' must remain remote and regal. Our 2IC believed that you cannot trust a man who does not drink (Buddha did not)- No 2 never took more than two *chota* (small drinks).

Officers Team -1955

We also had Capts Jasbir and Sekhon (two Patiala Sardars), who were determined to self-destruct for no better reason than competitive overdrinking. Both succeeded. Maj. Iqbal C. was a lovable *shikari (hunter)* and an angler and a soldiers' soldier. The trio of shining stars-Capts Jairam (basketball wizard) Rai Singh (staff college Camberley and MVC), and Raza (the nawab)- were supremely sophisticated, super-confident and suitably pompous. They could overwhelm any competition in smooth talk and trumpeting about Second to None!

But whither a 'mentor' for a minnow! The overworked cliché that the senior subaltern fulfills this role rarely works in field areas owing to constraints of continuity and availability. The art of regimental soldiering has to be learnt hands-on as it is rooted in each regiment's subculture and a local guru (mentor) is needed. The following incident is illustrative.

There was a firing range within our Base- the hillside facing POK served as the butt-end. During one of the live firing practices, I felt the need to enforce academy-style range drills. I was a bit overzealous in disciplining some sluggish soldiers, with rolls and hops cadet-style. Within hours, I was marched up before the CO and accused of kicking a *jawan's* butt. The Senior JCO had reported this to the Subedar Major, who had informed the CO. I was summarily banished to the highest Post with no right of response or appeal, with orders to move forthwith. I barely reached the top, after negotiating minefields, before nightfall.

Snowbound Post- Keeping fit

Investigations later revealed that while forward-rolling, the neck of his own water-bottle had poked the soldier in the back, and he assumed that the hollering hothead must have kicked his butt! I was exonerated later but stayed in the doghouse for months. My batman found out that it was a set-up by JCOs to teach the young upstart a lesson-. I must have ruffled some egos!

Is such intrigue a norm or exception within Units? In fixed-class Units (with sub-units of one class e.g. Jat and Dogra Coys as in my Battalion), insidious games like this are not uncommon. It is these cultural nuances that cannot be learnt from manuals. The handling of JCOs is another challenge for which YOs are not well equipped. Such challenges may seem as exclusive to military leadership, but human nature wears no uniform.

Wherever human interactions are involved awareness of such behavioural intricacies is invaluable.

My return to this area was nostalgic. There were local families and friends with whom we had broken bread, shared culture, customs and celebrations in complete disregard of religious differences. Call it Kashmiriyat or whatever you wish! The ladies sang the same *sangeet* (Punjabi folk), cracked common jokes and cared for each other's children.

A decade later, all social links and loyalties had become suspect. My dilemma was whether I should reflexively treat local families as hostile. Should a soldier react mechanically in such matters? To those dyed in the traditional wool of 'Theirs is not to reason why, /theirs is but to do and die', this may be a no-brainer! But it is a dharam-sankat (moral) issue for anyone with sensitivity, especially in the context of sub-conventional warfare based on identity conflicts!

Move to a Peace Station

During the year there had been a change of command and normal turnover of officers, including the 2IC. The new CO, Col (later Maj Gen) Prakash Grewal was a graceful, gregarious, and a high-calibre professional. He became a father figure for me as I worked closely with him as the Bn IO (Intelligence staff officer) and absorbed so much of his style and values.

After completion of our field tenure we moved to Babina as a part of the Armoured Brigade. A leap from the mountains into mechanised operations was exciting. The GRENADIERS had a history of operating with tank brigades during World War II and with the Lorried Brigade prior to induction in J&K.

We were then the only Motor Battalion of the Indian Army, with the role of providing close support to tanks when fighting through built-up areas and at night. We were part of the Black Elephant family, an elite strike formation of the Army. The cavalry- men are a special breed with a swagger all their own. They are passionate on the field of training, and off it! They take pride in high professional standards and scandals. Since WW-II they had seen little field service, and a peacetime soldier's mind can be a devil's workshop- here is an illustration!

Babina is a one-horse town with nothing more than the Army camp. All socialising is done at home or in Messes. On Diwali eve all Unit officers and families had assembled at the 2IC's residence. It was not far from the Flagstaff House, the Brigade Commander's official residence, where he was hosting cocktails for the COs. Suddenly there was a blast from that direction and a mad flurry ensued.

Our CO came rushing in and ordered battle stations for everyone. Someone had sent a primed grenade as a Diwali gift to the Commander, and it was hand-delivered during the cocktails. Fortunately, one of our NCOs was on duty and he recognised the grenade and the striker's sound. He reflexively threw the package out of the French window, before the grenade burst.

Despite 100% physical checks and intensive investigations, the details of the conspiracy remained buried except that it was internal intrigue by a disaffected clique. Our then commander was an upright professional who did not gel well with the prevailing cavalry culture. Not only was he wanting in major vices but he lacked even the minor ones, like wine, women, and wickedness! He was too disciplined and honest and did not overlook indiscretions. He was a Jain by faith, owned half a colony in Delhi, and held strongly to his ascetic values and ways!

But strong views provoke strong reactions. Perhaps some hotheads felt that misfits must be minimised, and that had become a motive for the incident. Many heads rolled for various lapses; lessons must have been learnt, but none publicly. The Army Chief threatened disbandment if there was a repeat but did not clarify whether he meant the armoured corps or the Division?

My point in telling this story is that power-plays of all shades exist in most human organisations and leaders have to learn to deal with them without damaging the fabric or essential ethos of the organisation. Regimental experience is the only learning ground for this.

We soon had a new Commander and he was 'steaming hot'. Brig (later Maj Gen.) Hari Badhwar was a charismatic professional, socially gifted and a perfect gentleman. He had joined the British army in the ranks, competed with the best and risen to this level. He was an international bridge player, an expert cook, and a gardening expert. One day while I, along with an equally clueless working party, was trying to re-lay the Mess lawn, he walked in. During the next hour, he gave us a tutorial-cum-demo on how to level a lawn with two wooden pegs, a plank and a spirit level. He taught us the right way to prepare the soil and plant the grass. There was no CO or other officer nor any fuss of formality all this time- how many higher commanders are like that?

He could socialise gracefully and scold with equal effect. An example of the latter is imprinted in my mind. During an exercise with troops, a situation was painted where tanks could not outflank the position and the Motor Battalion was tasked to punch a hole through the enemy position at night, so that tanks could go through the gaps and resume advance. My CO was handed over the situation at around 17:00 hours, and he gave his orders before last light. The attack and the infiltration went as planned. During the summing-up next day the Commander made some scathing comments about the Infantry's operation, based on an ill-informed umpire's feedback.

Prakash Grewal took umbrage and sulked for a whole week- no bridge or socialising with the Boss (they were thick as thieves earlier). When the Commander found out the reason, he directed that the same audience be assembled in our Unit. He apologised and hugged our CO publicly; we were all in tears! We had learnt a great lesson, by example: when the heart is without malice, misunderstandings have no place. There is grace in apology and forgiveness- as both symbolise strength not weakness! These two professional giants have left the largest footprint in my mind.

Next two years passed in normal peace-time activities of training, sports competitions, socialising and career courses. I managed to squeeze-in three Instructor level courses viz. Weapons, Physical training and mechanical transport (D&M). An anecdote related to pre-course culture is worth recounting. When detailed for the weapons-course at the Infantry School, I approached the Adjutant for pre-course training. He laughed and sent for the Courses register and pointed to results of the past- almost all average grades (CZ).

In an annoyed tone he asked 'Now you want to spoil this record? We don't want bloody Napoleons in this Battalion, only average regimental officers'. His logic seemed impeccable till I met those detailed for the same course in the Armoured Regiments. The bottom-line set for them was AX (I) (above average, fit for Instructor) grading and a full- scale dummy pre-course cadre was run to prepare them.

The GRENADIERS have since caught up with this culture of professional excellence. When a youngster hits the bull's eye, it tends to become his habit because he has proved to himself that 'He can!' It is such boosters that push up YOs trajectory into higher orbits- as it did for me. I recall my CO proudly taking me to the Brigade Commander after an exceptional performance on the Physical Training (PT) Course, to be personally complimented.

Two new subalterns had joined the Unit by now- Lts. Walia and Harbaksh Singh. Both were highly talented and mustard keen! Walia was gifted in sports and socially and Harbaksh was a hockey Olympian. Normally clever competition from juniors can be unsettling but I was so secure by now as to keep them 'at heel'! Sadly at this time, we lost one of the finest but flawed team-mates. Capt Raj Sekhon of 1st Course NDA was a handsome specimen of manhood, a hockey and athletics blue from IMA and extremely popular with All Ranks and the women.

His alcohol-dependence had crossed all tolerable limits which left the CO with no choice but to post him out on adverse report. He had successfully subverted all attempts at persuasion or control- the *laxman-rekha* was crossed when during stock taking of mess liquor a deficiency of 60 scotch-bottles and 105 tins of Gold Flake cigarettes were discovered.

Raj had won-over the Abdar (Bar in-charge) and conspired with him to keep serving him incognito drinks during the ban on his drinking.

During my leave later that year, I went to meet him in his new unit, which was stationed near Jammu. True to his form he had put everyone in a spin. A tanga (Horse cart) driver and his horse had been put in the Quarter-guard by his order for asking payment for his ride back from town, after a drinking binge. Raj was shunted out by the CO, Col. Kim Yadav to 3 GRENADIERS in Nagaland and thence into ultimate oblivion by another martinet CO, Stan Menezes, who was later the Vice Chief and Colonel The GRENADIERS. It is a sad story but Raj reaped what he had sown for himself!

Move to GAZA

There was a spate of postings- own officers reverting to regimental duty and a few coming in from other Units. The churning culminated in a change of command with our CO and the Centre Commandant changing places. All this was a precursor for our move for a foreign assignment with the United Nations Emergency Force in Gaza, Egypt.

I had just completed a course at the Army School of Mechanical Transport (ASMT) and was the logical choice for the advance party as handing/taking over of vehicles was involved. The 2IC was the leader of the team, with Capts Tony Michigan and Raza as other members. We were airlifted in an Air India chartered flight during mid 1958. The Air Hostesses pampered us with good food and drinks resulting in some pretty weak-kneed and bilious faces on landing at El Arish airport in Sinai Peninsula.

We were inducted a few months in advance of the main body so as to fully familiarise and take over duties from the incumbent Parachute Battalion. Their CO was the celebrated, Lt Col (later GOC-in-C) Inder Gill, MC. His quirky life and command style are the stuff of military folklore. I have not met a more eccentric and outstanding professional- a true military genius; nor seen a more spirited team of officers and fighting-fit men. This Unit is now a proud part of our elite Special Forces.

Our stay with them was a learning experience of good things and mad. The half Sikh-Scot Inder Gill would drink and socialise for twelve to fourteen hours a day (crunching his drinking-glass after midnight) and yet was in complete control of his command. He would briefly attend office- giving his command guidance on little notes, stuck on a nail, which his **personal staff** would carry to the Adjutant next morning. Only the crazy can dream of emulating his style- such a commander is a one-time mould of the Maker!

We drove across the Sinai to visit Cairo and Alexandria. We also visited the Pyramids, the battlefield of El Alamein and the towns along the Suez Canal and Sinai- as a part of area familiarisation and for liaising with the Embassy and Egyptian authorities. Exploring night clubs and Egyptian culture (belly-dancing) was a part of the taking-over process. Capt Raza was a reluctant observer on grounds of his freshly-married (and father-to-be) status-later he sacrificed his Europe leave to receive his son Maroof's delivery. Tony and I were able to do a re-run of the Exodus in the footsteps of Moses, including a visit to the top of Mount Sinai. Ancient civilisations and antiquities have since been a passion.

GAZA BEACH-1959

I have already recounted the personal and romantic side of my UNEF story. That tenure was not merely a 'courtship' trip but also a rich professional experience. Besides peacekeeping operations along the

Armistice Demarcation Line, we competed most favourably with six other Contingents, in all arenas- professional, sports and social, except in their special strengths (e.g. Brazilians thrashed us in football, as also the Yugoslavs and Swedes). And the Scandanavians always got the better of us in beer-drinking and the Yugoslavs in schnapp toasting!

Our star performers were our athletes and the hockey team under Harbaksh. They were the top draw in UNEF and much in demand for exhibition matches all over Egypt. An officers' demonstration on patrolling and ambushes was highly commended by the Force Commander, Gen Burns of Canada. He had commanded an Armoured Division in war and had a fetish for testing MT mobility during inspections. He would order the fleet to move out for a long drive and check the breakdowns or laggards. I was the MTO and my Team excelled during his inspections.

But there was a flip-side to our Gaza tenure viz the 'gold-rush' for attractive PX items. There was a greedy clique that was systematically collecting the loot for gifting, and this virus had infected the ranks. I got a taste when a Jawan (soldier), who had collected multiple gadgets on my authorisation, offered to sell one back in Ambala (to satisfy a pesty cousin) at three times its price. Such money-mindedness is toxic for a fighting unit's ethos.

While many multiplied money, my collection was a silver medal in Squash, gold in bridge tournament and a priceless fiancée (to follow). Only Lt Walia came back with less- just a red sports-cycle acquired from Aden. We also relish a heapful of happy memories of our joint-trip to Europe.

Return to Ambala

By end of December 1959, we were back in Ambala Cantonment. Many VIP visits followed for a pat and some for goody collection. It is indeed worldly-wise to invest in career advancement, but there is a Master's red flag that says 'Do your duty and don't mess with my design'! Many manipulated benefits were reversed sooner than later.

The moral of this story is that the cycle of 'sowing and reaping' is inescapable! There is always a payback time for those who stray, tempted by flesh or fortune. The flawed but faithful, like me, came out smiling! And I don't just mean faithful to a 'fiancée' but values and virtues that count.

The epic-battlefield of Mahabharata is not far from Ambala. The year 1960 turned out to be my Kurukshetra (ancient site of the epic battle of Mahabharata). My CO had taken umbrage over my indiscreet remark during a conference and also discovered my flawed lineage- as the son of the acerbic Engineer who had refused his request for extra water connections, when he was posted on staff in Jammu. He had endorsed a negative recommendation on my application for marriage permission and resignation letter.

I survived and succeeded. In 1988 while I was commanding an Infantry Division in Ferozepur, we both went out of our way to call on that old CO, with all deference due to an Elder. He was in deep dementia by then but his eyes lit up with affection on seeing us. It is such encounters that make one realise the futility of rancour or negativity and the virtue of compassion and love in human, including Regimental, relations. It needs a lifetime to understand human nature and learn leadership. The first part of that learning experience began for me in the Battalion that I was commissioned into viz the SECOND TO NONE!

CHAPTER 3

Rounding- Off Regimental Experience

Despina had flown into Bombay a few days ahead of me (owing to air-reservation problems) and was received by a former UNEF colleague, Maj Jaywant and his wife. After a pleasant transit halt she reached Delhi where she was received by an old friend, Lt Walia. By last week of Aug I had joined her and we reached the Unit in Ambala after a short visit to Jammu, where she was warmly welcomed as per traditional customs.

We rotated our ad-hoc stay between guest rooms in Sirhind Club, Officers Mess and homes of officers proceeding on leave. Capt (later Brig) Rai, MVC and Savita generously allowed us to stay for over a month in their home during their leave. I made myself so much at home as to serve his scotch while entertaining friends - he refused to be compensated!

Despina was well known in the Unit and was fondly embraced and assimilated in the Unit family. Her comfort level with unit families caught the watchful eye of the Brigade Commander during an athletics meet. He checked if sanction for my marriage had come. The negative response prompted him to endorse an adverse remark in my Annual Report 'this officer is living in sin, pending formal Army sanction'! I laughed it off as I had already resigned!

My first Indian gift to Despina was an Eastern-Star cycle which made her as mobile as I was. We would pedal across (or under) the rail-road bridge to go for a game of squash, swim or for the evening dance at the Club. We trekked and went on adventure rides to Corbusier's Chandigarh, on borrowed bikes of unit officers. Life was like a fairy tale and a blast of fun- despite the Damocles-sword of my resignation.

I was surprised to receive orders of posting as an Instructor at an Army training establishment. Regimental soldiering is the foundation but a balanced career profile needs instructional and staff exposures. But this was an unusual assignment for an Infantry officer- a cross between a military-transport manager and an auto-engineer's job. My bull-dog instinct was ready for a fight even on this technical front! Many a Regimental luminary (Generals Airy, Kahlon, Ghosh and Nagpal) later followed me in this job but it was a first for a Grinder then!

I had to send Despina to Jammu to stay with my parents when I proceeded on posting. It turned out to be an invaluable opportunity for her to bond with the family. I was needlessly concerned about adjustment issues due to language and culture variables. Where there is goodwill there is God's grace!

In later years she would fondly reminisce about my Mother's *'aarti'* *(prayer)* time. She admired her singing and harmonium-playing and found the rhythm of 'Om *Jai Jagdish Hare*' (closing prayer) to be soul-stirring. My younger Brothers would take turns to drive her to the Chapel for Sunday Mass- two of them are ex students of that Convent.

Ma Ji with the family and pets,
in our lawn

Her messing-around in the kitchen, while seated on the ground, and speed-knitting were the envy of all ladies. She had knitted a cardigan for everyone before re-joining me. A touching moment was when my father ticked-off a guest who hesitated in accepting food offered by her: 'She is my daughter. Anyone not comfortable with food offered by her is not welcome'. Despina had lost her father early in life-a paternal-figure filled a deep need! Ever since, her ties with my kin have been closer than mine!

Formal approval for our marriage was received and all problems were resolved by the first week of Dec. She joined me on 10 Dec, duly escorted by my Grandfather (Nana Ji), wearing a low-slung revolver and a vigilant eye during the long train journey to Faizabad!

Our three years in that God-forsaken place were blissful and highly productive. We lived in a huge colonial bungalow of eight rooms with a row of staff-quarters occupied by a bevy of domestic staff- a maid, gardener, water-carrier, sweeper, and rickshaw-puller; all willing to work part-time on token-payment. Our daily needs were taken good care of by this team of service providers.

There was no running water or wet-sanitation. A bullock cart delivered drinking water and for other needs there was a well. It was a culture-shock for her- even for me! But it was compensated by plenty of positives e.g. our togetherness, abundant domestic-help and facilities for fun and adventure like moon-lit boat-rides on Saryu River and a positively friendly-Faizabad! But the finest-feature was the well-knit officer's team!

Most of us were contemporaries from Academy days- a bunch of high-calibre devils! The fact that at the end most of us rose to be General officers (worth 20 stars plus) speaks for itself. Most of us were newly married and all our first-borns are of that vintage. But we also worked hard and played tough to maintain our professional reputations.

Initially it was a real grind but after teaching two courses one could breeze through. I acquired a scooter which enabled us to explore the sights, history and culture of Central India. It was beyond our wildest imagination then that one day I would be the C in C of Central Command.

Ayodhya, a pilgrimage node, was only a few kilometers away. We hosted a horde of guests and had become fairly competent tourist guides. I recall our stopping short on seeing a plaque 'Non-Hindus not allowed' at Hanuman-Garhi temple. The head Priest saw that and waved both of us up! Those were truly secular times.

A joy-ride to Lucknow was a fortnightly feature. An early start on Sunday morning enabled catching the morning English movie at Mayfair, a Chinese lunch, a Hindi matinee show followed by filter-coffee at India Coffee House. Having logged nearly 300 KMs we would return late at night- could it get crazier? Soon this madness had to stop owing to Despina's pregnancy.

An SOS call came from my Brother-in-law, Maj Magotra, beckoning Despina to Jhansi for my Sister's delivery as no one could come from Jammu. Despite her own status she responded like a trooper. She was present right through the delivery and when she ran out with the good news 'Beautiful Baby–girl', the good Doctor was crest-fallen. He could not resist the Son-Syndrome due to social/family pressure! My sister impulsively suggested '*Bhabhi,* if you have a son, let us exchange!' Despina nodded but when the suggestion was raised after Arun was born the fiercely possessive Greek Mother turned 'deaf' to any deal!

Now it was her turn to have the baby. My ex Regimental Medical Officer (RMO) of Uri days was in command of the Section Hospital (a mini Military Hospital). During a pre-natal check the probability of breech-presentation arose, which reduced the chances of a normal delivery and that would need specialist care. I requested my Mother to come down and she obliged...

Some weeks later there were disturbing symptoms and Maj Pal advised immediate evacuation to Command Hospital in Lucknow. He ruled out a bumpy road journey by ambulance and followed up with a creative solution – evacuation by train with Nursing staff and emergency kit. She was evacuated in a cabin of a goods train. I followed up by road and found another ex 2nd Bn RMO, of Gaza days, to host me for a month. Such is the stuff of Grinder spirit!

My Mother was left alone at Faizabad to pray- and she did that, by daily lighting a candle at the altar as she had seen done. She would pray to the Divine (mercifully multi-lingual) in her own words!

On 3 Mar 62, after 18 hours of hard-labour, the baby was delivered by caesarian section. Our bonny-baby had lost her way at entry-point. The Nursing officers consoled the young Mother 'she has given you enough pain for a life-time!' For the euphoric Mother nothing mattered except her bundle of joy! I know little about pains in-between but the same Baby kept clinging to the Mother till her last breath, paying-back a little of the love she had received; while her Son and I stood as speechless spectators!

We gave our girl a double-barreled name, Athena Anuradha. Ever since my visit to Athens I was fascinated by the imagery of the warrior-goddess of wisdom- a mix of Saraswati and Kali! And Despina had loved the tender sound of Anuradha, a character in a movie of same name! We have believed in 'mix and match' as the way to integrate divergences!

In Oct 62, the Chinese invaded our Northern borders and humiliated a naive India. Our badly deployed forces bore the brunt bravely but crumbled. Sadly my ex CO of Gaza days, a newly promoted Brigadier, became a casualty of that debacle.

At this time the famous writer Vidya Naipaul and his British wife were guests of a Cambridge educated IAS friend. Our boasts before them about 'bloody nose' to the Chinese, based on All India Radio reports, blew up in our face. Mercifully Naipaul did not include that in his in-famous book 'An Area of Darkness'. Moral of the story: do not trust official reports!

But the after-shock hit us harder. Battle Physical Efficiency Tests (BPETs) were ordered to be conducted every quarter for All Ranks. Normally these are an annual feature and rarely enforced at Training Establishments. At last, serious preparations were being started by us after the war was over!

Our Comdt implemented the new policy with Japanese-rigour- he had been a Jap POW for many years! He even added a few knife-twists of his own- all Ranks will be tested together and results will be posted on Notice–boards! This was a set-up for humiliation. Nandu Srivastava and I, both young Captains from fighting Arms, took the challenge head-on. We will lead the pack or drop-dead trying. We were young, fit and reckless.

For next four quarters we reserved the 1-2 slots between us, despite challenges from younger Jawans and NCOs. Later we would race each other to better our own timings. The cycle-borne Comdt took cognisance and reflected it in our Reports (ACR). I attribute my selection for Ranger Course (commando training) in USA to this recognition of our madness!

In my third year as Instructor I was allotted a vacancy for a course in Pune. When I called on Maj Shete, VrC of 2nd Bn, who was posted in Command HQ at Pune, he arranged temporary family accommodation and offered full-time use of his scooter! I promptly sent for the family. The long journey from Faizabad to Poona with a nursing Baby and no reservation was a nightmare. Such is an Army wife's lot!

Snowbound Dalhousie- 1964
Athena, Despina and Me
on the Right (front)

Thereafter we made the most of our stay- when others were sweating we would ride, roam and relax. This relaxed attitude and receptive mind enabled me to steal an A (Instr) grade despite fierce competition. No one had been awarded an 'A' for years on this course, even amongst the current crop of Instructors. Moral of the story: relaxed tortoises can beat hypertensive hares!

Regimental Posting to 8 GRENADIERS

In late 1963 I was posted to 8 GRENADIERS, a newly raised Battalion located at Dalhousie. I protested about change of panel but was given a 'shut up call' by Colonel The GRENADIERS. His stern response 'I cannot import officers for our new-raisings? I have personally selected you for this unit'. That last bit is a standard pacifier. The good news was that married accommodation was available at the new station.

Dalhousie is a heavenly hill station. I shared a cute all-wood cottage with three Grinder families. There was a coal-fed fire place for warmth during snow-bound months- a first-time experience for both my Girls!

The CO was a highly sophisticated professional. He had already commanded 3 GRENADIERS. There had been problems during that command so he was given a second-chance. The officers' team was a mixed bag with a pack of raw YOs, mostly Emergency Commissioned (ECOs) – some were middle aged and others needed baby-sitting!

I was given command of A Company comprising of Jat troops- many from my old Bn. My challenge was to knit the disparate group into a cohesive combat-team. I had two ECOs as Coy Officers- Tau Malhan (a 35 year old former school-teacher) and Kelly Boy (he was a state-level badminton play-boy).

After the intense BPETs in Faizabad I was in peak physical form. The way to a Jat's heart is via personal example of toughness, followed by robust rough-talk. I set a scorching pace in both. We would run down to Banikhet (5 KMs one way) and back; and then from atop a rock I would yell at anyone lagging behind! They loved it- *'key sher sa gaje se, be** Ch**', (how he roars like a lion, bloody SO*)*. After my recent course, I was on steroids for training by camping out - Majs Hada and Balu Brar would happily tag their Coys to train with me. We would march to and back from Pathankote (50 kms one way) for plains-warfare and Kala-Tope for mountain-operations. Our Formation was dual-tasked!

The Brigade got detailed for a new task viz. to act as enemy for a Mountain Division in all operations of war. The Exercise would last for 2-3 months in Sugar Sector, near Hindustan-Tibet border.

The incumbent Adjutant had to go for a career-course and I was asked to fill-in. The CO agreed to my request that I should continue to command my Coy when tasked. This two-sided exercise with troops was an amazing training experience. I shall skip the details, except to relate two incidents.

As per Exercise-narrative, the enemy's invasion had been contained and opposing forces were facing each other across a deep valley. An arrogant Colonel from Control HQ came with a special-mission viz. to simulate an out-flanking attack on the defender's depth-localities with a Coy group (to represent a Redland Regt i.e. a Bde). It involved going down the River valley, climbing and crossing two ridge-lines and executing an outflanking move of 30-40 KMs in 48 hrs.

Survival training

My CO laughed at the unrealistic tasking and gave cogent reasons. The Colonel from Control HQ asked 'Are you refusing to accept the task?' This was getting overheated between two Sardars. I took the CO aside and suggested 'Sir let us take it, with some changes'. The Old Man was sceptical 'Who will do it?' I volunteered with assurance of my best-shot!

We surprised everyone by reaching the objective 6 hrs ahead of schedule, undetected by live surveillance elements. Suddenly 8 GRENADIERS became the toast of the Corps, Control HQ and professionals on both sides. Lesson learnt- 'Even competent leadership needs supportive teamwork'. Soldiering is not a gladiators-game; but a calculated gamble! During 1965 war the same CO did not gamble and still lost.

The other story is personal. I suspected that my Coy staff were covering up something- it was a tiny Tibetan-pup; *'Baby ji ke liye hai, Sahib (It is for Athena Baby, Sir)!'* was the sheepish confession. Earlier they had gifted her a little lamb, which had overgrown! Such is the spirit that bonds a Regimental family- and it is a very precious asset!

Rangers Course in USA

A surprise gift arrived for me in early 65. I was selected for the Ranger Course at US Army Infantry School, Fort Benning. The local consensus was that it must be all about firing ranges; till a cdo-qualified Young Officer informed us that Rangers were the US version of Commandos!

RANGERS

Raj Bahuguna (later Maj Gen), an illustrious course-mate was also selected. He was a high-flyer, covered in sports-blues from top to toe and one of the toppers of my course. Four Indian officers had attended this course earlier and two had suffered fracture injuries. A 50% survival rate and a fierce competition this time seemed scary - but the prospect of a trip to US made it worth it!

Ranger training is designed to be 'highest standard of practical field training'. This was a training imperative for the US Army in 1965. US Army's involvement in Vietnam was at its peak then. They were a National service non-volunteer Army then and there was rapid turnover of manpower. Hence the cutting-edge of tactical level

Survival training

leaders had to be combat-conditioned, physically and psychologically, as rapidly as possible. There was no better instrument than Ranger-Airborne training for that. It enables trainees to test depths of their physical and mental endurance and pushes them to limits of tolerance-thresholds. The Ranger-Airborne tab was the ultimate symbol of the macho military-man in the US.

All our 175 course-mates (Americans and 20 plus Allied students) were highly motivated and tense (but in some ways less skilled than us- we had 10 years service experience compared to their 3-7). But in the ultimate analysis, all soldiers are the same—rugged and resilient fighters. It was an intense training experience; and we felt satisfied to have left a stamp of high professionalism.

We both qualified creditably and I was declared an Honour Graduate-Raj never forgave me for upstaging a course-superior. My view: he tried too hard while a tenacious tortoise got ahead!

Honour Graduate -
RANGERS, USA - 1965

On the way back from Fort Benning, Georgia, I travelled via New York, London, Athens to Cairo-Ismailia to spend time with family and friends. These photographs were taken during those transit halts. On return I was posted as a senior instructor at Commando Wing of the Infantry School at Mhow. That story follows.

With family in New York

Despina's Uncle & Aunt

CHAPTER 4

Commando Dagger To Counter-Insurgency

20, Generals Road, Mhow-1965. Despina and Athena with Ms Lopez,our landlady,

While I was in the US, Despina stayed with my Sister in Delhi, as 8 GRENADIERS got deployed. Pakistan had launched infiltrators to stoke insurgency in J&K. A feint attack had earlier taken place in Kutch Sector in which my parent unit viz. 2nd Bn which was based in Bombay was involved.

On our return from the US in July 65, Raj and I were both posted as Commando (Cdo) Instructors in Mhow. The criticality and context of cdo training in India was comparable to that in the US. Consequent to Sino-Indian clash of 1962, Indian Army had to be modernized and expanded three-fold. The assembly-lines of officer-training were churning-out hordes of YOs. War-clouds were again building-up in 1965. The cutting edge of our combat-leadership had to be sharpened very fast. Cdo training was the best way of doing that.

We had barely settled down in the new station when orders came for a five-fold expansion of cdo training courses. It is easy for intentions to be bold and elastic but training infrastructure and human-resources are not so flexible! The trained pool of qualified instructors was thin and the infrastructure e.g. cdo target areas, firing ranges, obstacle courses etc were a major constraint. Even local availability of live-snakes for survival training was doubtful. It was indeed an ambitious and challenging target calling for creative solutions.

It is in times like this that the commando-credo of: 'when the going gets tough the tough get going' and the 'impossible only takes a little longer' is tested! Our Commander was a peripatetic paratrooper who had been instrumental in post 62 revival of jungle warfare and commando training. Col (later GOC-in-C) Tirath Oberoi was a professional workaholic, utterly indefatigable and yet a deeply human leader. He led a team of highly motivated professionals, even before we had joined!

We had to pull every rabbit out of our creative-hats and put together a new structure and system to implement this expansion. And this is how we did that. Instead of one batch of 175 trainees, we planned to run five courses of 35, with a stagger of one week each. This way we could rotate training areas, facilities and infrastructure. To replenish the Instructor's pool we ran crash courses for all-comers with potential, without compromising quality. Later, we set up our own snake-farm-more about it later.

Our Cdr was never off-duty- he had no other interest in life. As Senior Instructors we took 12 hourly shifts and yet had to strain to keep up with him. But he had some mindsets which, in our perception, detracted from realism of training. One such was an obsession with time-on target viz. all raids must go within scheduled timings! If not, it would be a poor reflection on our training standards, especially in the eyes of VIPs/visitors. Consequently, the duty instructors were inclined to give covert guidance to lost/off-track missions. There would be no one to do so in real war- during Rangers we were allowed to get lost and learn lessons from it; and we did!

Secondly, he had a fetish for raising physical benchmarks of individual performance e.g. jump heights, speed-march timings etc. One wondered whether we were training gladiators/circus performers or Cdo teams for operations. We had seen sustained stress/psychological pressure disable the best e.g. freezing up on cliff-edges or high-wires or suffer a breakdown due to cumulative stress.

Later Col Sallick, VrC, took over command. His style was softer but as inspiring. Both Raj and I were eligible to take the next Staff College

Entrance Examination- being younger I stood down. He qualified and left and I followed next year.

During my second year I had to undertake an interesting visit to Bombay. It was to study snake farming at the Haffkine Institute where anti-venin vaccine is made. I wanted to go by scooter as I was unlikely to get official transport for this duty. Despina was five months pregnant yet adamant on accompanying. Four of us (one in the pouch) on the scooter, with all our baggage made quite a sight. It rained on the way and I had a tyre-burst- but it was all worth it. All is well that ends well-as Col Nazareth, a senior Grinder, commented after our return 'Yogi should be shot and Despina given a Gold-medal'.

Roadies Enroute to Bombay - 1966

A few months later, our son Arun was born in the Military Hospital. He was overdue so we decided to go on a bumpy ride to induce delivery- she was determined not to have an operation this time. When we returned, there was panic in the MH- An In- patient missing without permission. I sneaked her in and exfiltrated quietly like a good cdo, and resurfaced only after the delivery. Cdo Instructors were suspected of suffering from mad-cow syndrome! A week earlier Capt Ojha our Medical Officer, had nearly died due to snake bite of our pet-cobra- it had been defanged but had re-grown roots.

DSSC Wellington- Officers Mess function

Meanwhile I qualified for the 1967 Staff Course at Wellington. Five years later I was posted as a Directing Staff (Instructor) – I must have done well on the course. I shall skip details of this phase except to flag the essence of staff training. Just as Ranger-Cdo training enables one to plumb one's psycho-physical depths, staff course does the same for one's professional-intellectual horizons. The interaction with the 'cream of contemporaries' and very high-calibre faculty (in-house and guest) is truly empowering and expansive. It holds up a professional mirror to see one's comparative worth. It is an exceptional opportunity for professional growth.

It was hard work and also much fun and games. Despina took active part in dramatic activities. While I was busy in a war-game, she suffered an attack of glaucoma resulting in severe loss of vision. A neighbour's wife evacuated her to the nearest eye-specialist in a private hospital. I sent an SOS for my Mother and she came down to take care of the babies. Gradually her vision improved- the treating Lady Doctor became a lifelong friend. Many friends had kept praying for her recovery- they suggested visits to Tirupati and the Shrine at Vailankani (India's Lourdes). We did go to both for thanksgiving. It has helped and we have always believed that 'prayer is powerful'!

After the course I was posted as Second in Command (2IC) of 8 GRENADIERS in field area. The family was shifted back to Mhow from Wellington, and left in the care of former Cdo wing colleagues.

My Unit was deployed along the Line of Control in J&K when I joined. It was later rotated within the command for high-altitude tenure in Ladakh. Both these tenures were full of challenging experiences. There are so many anecdotal nuggets of the time but time, space and patience constrain one from sharing- except a few.

My CO proceeded on leave on the day I arrived. The GOC of the Division, Maj Gen Raina, MVC (later Chief), had conceptualized an exercise to test an operational concept involving counter-attack with pooled Units from widely scattered sectors. The Bn was nominated to participate under my command. We rehearsed multiple contingency plans involving long cross country moves (over 30 KMs). On D day, heavens opened up and it poured, resulting in the River enroute becoming unsafe for crossing. Without link-up, Exercise Khooni-Badla, would be an abortion; not on my watch! Despite Umpire's warning we risked a crossing- all officers had volunteered when asked. During the summing up next day the GOC complimented and declared that our performance had been most commendable but he also added that 'such risks can earn a medal or a court-martial'.

After I had earned two criteria reports in 8 GRENADIERS, I was posted as Brigade Major of a Brigade engaged in counter-insurgency operations in Nagaland. For administrative reasons I shifted the family to Lucknow. This was considered a good time for Despina and children to visit her Sisters in Australia. We were poorly paid and the field-area allowance was a pittance; but we were masters of deficit financing and a 'fly now pay later' plan' came to my rescue.

I took over the Brigade Major's assignment from my Regimental name-sake, Maj (later Lt Gen) Yogi Tomar. The newly raised Bde Group had been recently inducted from Trivandrum. It had no experience in counter insurgency operations and was led by a risk-averse Brigade

Commander. Despite being deployed in the heartland of underground hostiles (ANGAMI area) we were yet to open our score.

Unfortunately two of our patrols were ambushed by Naga Hostiles resulting in many casualties, including officers. We did not lose our heads but the 'revenge fuse' had been lit! A bold new Commander was posted in- he had been my DS at the Staff College. His personal courage and risk-taking were inspiring but, at times, on the wild side. In 1971 War he won an MVC (the second highest gallantry award) in command of the same Bde; and was then court-martialled as Maj Gen.

He unleashed our energies and sat-back in support. His command guidance to me was simple 'sub-unit level counter-insurgency operations are not my staple or level. I know you from Staff College and have confidence in you- handle these at your level and keep me informed'! His aggressive yet decentralized policy soon started to give results.

And then one day disaster struck. During a major cordon and search operation one of our combing parties crossed the killing-area of GHQ hideout of the underground Naga Army. It was ambushed and seriously mauled. All our men were killed except one who pretended to be dead.

Later, I was a witness to this tele-conversation between the GOC and my Cdr:-

> 'GOC: Army HQ wants to know whose head should roll for this incident?
>
> Cdr: Sir, I take full responsibility as the Bde Cdr, so it should be mine!
>
> GOC: Don't try to be a bloody hero, Hardev. I have already offered mine!'

Neither was playing to the gallery. Gen Zoru Bakshi had won an MVC in 1965 war and was one of the finest combat commanders. This conversation left a lasting impact on me- leadership is learnt from such role-models. I felt specially blessed that day.

Let me recount a different experience. We had successfully ambushed and captured a self-styled (SS) Bn Cdr of underground Naga Army with his armed escort. We had waited patiently for this prize catch. We knew that he visited his family in a village not far from my HQ. When I informed the Bde Cdr in the Mess, his reaction was 'Shoot the B...ds and show it as attempted escape'. I did nothing for a while and he asked why? I pushed a copy of the Time Magazine in front of him. It had the cover story of Lt Calley of US Army who had been indicted for cold-blooded murders in Viet Nam. And added 'Sir, asking an Indian soldier to commit murder is giving him a license to turn his gun in any direction'. He smiled and let it pass.

I kept (Self Styled Col) Kedopu Angami and his family in safe custody within the Bde camp. They were given full-scope witness–protection. After sustained interrogation he broke and gave us valuable intelligence about camps and caches of arms that led to disintegration of a Bn - any day a better deal than two dead bodies and a court-case.

For the next two years, the Bns of 95 Mtn Bde were declared the Best Battalions of 8 Mtn Div, based on operational results. 31 GUARDS and 1/11 GR won this honour for themselves and us!

The purpose of telling these stories is to illustrate the value of experience in 'rounding-off' one's professional personality. During these ten years (1960-70) I had held chequered appointments and competed with the best at home and abroad. I had attended the prestigious staff-course; taught technical subjects (at ASMT) and trained commandos; and done some crazy things. I claim credit only for never resisting a challenge and welcoming any assignment as a proving trial! None of us can predict results/rewards of one's effort - then why worry? That was the main lesson of this phase of my life.

The 'Powers that be' felt that I was now fit to command my parent-unit. In our days that was the ultimate professional aspiration of Regimental Officers. The thrills and traumas of command follow next.

CHAPTER 5

Battalion Command And Beyond

Taking over command is like summiting a peak. The challenge is in the climb and command-tenure is its culmination, especially if it is in battle. Instead of a chronology of events, I shall share my thoughts, from CO-designate till evacuation from an enemy-minefield- as perceived 45 years later. These are my reflections, not a 'cut and paste' from war-diary. It is a maverick's perspective, not history- absolutely no fabrications but some heretical thoughts in hindsight!

Commanding Officer -1970

My promotion and posting to 2 GRENADIERS came while I was a Brigade-Major in Nagaland. The mental preparations started straightaway. I searched for the best- practices of successful commanding officers (CO). Some role-models were shining examples of 'when I raise an eyebrow everyone within range should tremble', while others believed in 'earning respect without fear'! The ideal-template of a good CO is uniquely personal and context-based. But two variables are critical viz. combat-potential of the Unit and the ability of the leader to make it better.

I received the Unit brochure which contained all the information about its fighting-status. But the 'spirit' of a unit is more than data in a brief- it is a synergy of many intangibles. One has to experience it to know that reality!

My family was delighted at the prospect of a peaceful tenure at Bangalore. The Battalion (Bn) had earned a good station as a reward for the success and sacrifices during 1967 Nathu-la clash with the Chinese. On our way to Bangalore, we stopped at Madras (now Chennai) to meet my former CO and the serving Colonel the GRENADIERS, Gen. Prakash Grewal. It was a warm reunion but he roundly admonished me for indicating preference for command of 8 GRENADIERS, with words to the effect, 'this disloyal ba.....d, from my Team, wanted to command some other Unit!' I dared not explain that while the 200 year old 2nd Bn had nurtured my baby–steps, we had seeded the foundation of the 8th with our 'sweat and tears'-it was our 'baby'. In any case both were family! His parting advice was intriguing: "Buy up all the Kiwi polish in the Canteen, you have a lot of polishing to do; and don't spare my son." Their youngest son, Darshi Grewal was a YO in the Unit. He was my Adjutant during the71 War and rose to the rank of a Lt Gen. Sadly he died in harness, essentially due to a 'typical' lifestyle problem!

On arrival I found a well-knit and happy Unit. My predecessor, Col. P.P. Singh, had known both of us since Gaza days. He had charisma, social graces and was a popular leader. I did not know then that he was a Raja (ruler) of a tiny state called Bithoor near Kanpur. Many years later, when he suffered a heart attack at his farm and needed evacuation to Delhi I made all arrangements but it was the Army Commander's wife, Despina, who was glued to the phone to monitor his progress till he was handed over to a cardiologist in Delhi!

PP's popularity inspired fierce personal loyalty. He had to import the 2IC, Vikas Kochhar from the 3rd and some other officers of his choice, due to casualties suffered during Nathu-La operation. Such bonds can be very strong and personal. I felt the need to curb extra-territorial loyalty and gossip. All officers and families were invited for tea and offered an option to 'feel free to follow the leader-of-choice'. I promised to facilitate the posting. Nobody took the offer. I dealt likewise with symptoms of clan-based cliques in the Unit, a bane of the class-based Regiments. Team-building is a deliberate process-neither a birthright of a CO nor a function of populism. In hindsight, the cohesive-spirit of Team 71 is a shining spot of my career.

Despina played an invaluable role in this process. She compensated for my introverted nature with her warm, genuine and gregarious nature. Her approach to soldiers' family-welfare was so passionate that it inspired involvement and commitment - an incredible contrast to the pervasive dim view of the role of family welfare centre and Ladies' club.

CO & 2 IC Families with my Sub Maj
and Dvr- Bangalore - 1970

In her first visit to Family Lines she walked into the quarters of NCsE (Non-Combatants Enrolled) tradesmen like barbers, washer-men and safaiwalas (sanitary staff). She surprised a Safaiwala's wife with *'Tum mere ko chai nahin pilaogi (won't you offer me tea)'*? The innocent girl replied *'Aap mere ghar ki chai piyengi (will you drink my tea)*? Her response was *'Kyon nahin, agar saaf glass men do gi' (why not, provided you offer it in a clean glass)!*

That was not only endearing but a 'signal' that snowballed into a competitive drive for cleanliness, home-care and hygiene. It also served as a wake-up call for the class-conscious and some indifferent officers' wives!

Every such visit loaded the Quartermaster and the Medical Officer with a new wish list of maintenance and health-care issues. But she also believed in 'tough love' which won her lifelong loyalty of most but also hostility of some. Regimental bonding cannot come from the 'chain of command' only! The fabric of military ethos is woven through informal institutions or else it is notional!

During my meeting with the Commander (Cdr), he conveyed a cryptic signal, "Your Unit excels in administrative and social-skills; now build up its professional standards!" Both Gen. Grewal and the Brigadier admired PP- then where did the 'Kiwi-polish and change-of-tack' signals fit in? The Cdr's comment made sense in the context of reorientation from high altitude to desert operations. The Unit had earned laurels in the former but the latter is a different ball game.

My own baptism-by-fire came within a week during a Divisional level operational discussion. I was familiar with the Sinai and North African deserts and the boldness of Israeli military leaders. But I was innocent about our Thar desert-belt, along our Western border and our desert concepts. I saw no reason for our tactical thinking to be less bold; despite constraints e.g. few sand tyres?

My syndicate's plan must have reflected this thinking. It was selected for the 'rip-off'- it is also customary for the neck of the new kid to be put on the block! The vultures (other Syndicates) were unsparing in finding flaws. We defended gallantly and by the end of the day had won back some support amongst the 'brass.'

But I had misread the establishment line, which was to 'be conventional and conservative'! We retired hurt but not humbled and recouped at the bar. And that became a habit- more to project a macho image of hard-drinking and foul-mouthed fighting-men! So many have dug their grave pursuing that line too seriously!

The next challenge came when the General Officer Commanding (GOC) of the Division came to visit the Brigade. Gen. Mathur (later GOC-in-C) was a shining star from the Signals, who had the reputation of being a martinet-an iron-fist in a velvet glove! I let the Senior JCO's do the ground-work for the VIP visit- 75 % of my younger officers had less than 3 years' service. It was also infra-dig for COs of the time to have dry runs.

The GOC arrived and killed our preparations. He directed that the Unit be assembled centrally and nominated the front-rank for snap-shooting test on the firing range; the centre-rank for a 2-mile battle-run; and rear for a tricky rope-test. It was a smart way to generate a random-sample but the results of selective testing cannot tally with the records. GOC felt pleased at having exposed us but our Brigade Commander was livid.

Next day all COs tried to explain to the Cdr that selective surprise tests do not represent true standards. We suggested that the GOC be invited to re-test after six weeks. I had trained commandos in less time than that! He did invite and the GOC came-this time he pulled out a new rabbit. He swept the stores, langars and loos with a fine-tooth comb for any cobwebs- physical or mental! Much later I learnt of a 'game people play' called NIGY-SOB (Now I Got You S**!) Gen. Mathur was definitely not playing that- it was beneath his class. But I know many senior officers addicted to it! I resolved (and hopefully followed) that 'showing the flag' by higher Cdrs must be for up-lifting spirits, not depressing a Unit!

But my spirits were not uplifted when my Unit came second in Brigade athletics and featured in fewer podium finishes during Regimental Reunion of Dec 70. Notwithstanding the high-altitude tenure and unsettled status since, this was unbecoming of the senior-most Battalion of the Regiment.

Families of CO and 2IC at Bde Acquatics Meet

A total turn-around had to be achieved. In less than a year we were the Divisional champions in most professional and sports competitions. But other challenges loomed on the horizon throughout 1971, culminating in the War.

During winter months we moved to Rajasthan for extensive desert training. We honed our battle-drills and desert skills to a level that the Chief Umpire was moved to pay an enviable compliment "This Unit's battle-drills and desert skills are comparable to the best demonstrations of the Infantry School!"

Kochhar was posted out and my old buddy, Maj Walia, joined as Second-in-Command (2IC). Being No. 2 is a challenge anytime, as managing expectations both ways is never easy. But the aptly named Manmohan Walia handled a maverick CO and a 'wild-bunch' very well.

Operation Torchlight in Ceylon

On a Sunday in Mar '71, I got a telephonic warning-order from the Southern Army Commander. It was for an SOS mission to Ceylon (now Sri Lanka) where left-wing extremists had almost taken over the Island. I was to fly-out with a vanguard-group, pending further buildup.

The Army Commander's cryptic call said, "You know about the trouble brewing further south. The Lady down-under has sought help from our Lady (referring to respective Prime Ministers). How soon can you get going?" I gave him my best estimate-within an hour of the air-lift being provided.' Within hours, the skeleton Battalion HQ (with Atma as my staff officer) and D Company group (with Dalbir and Dahiya) were airborne for Katunayake Air Force Base near Colombo. Our Air Force did a fine job of landing us in a frozen void. The aircraft had to quickly turn-around after offloading, as the ground security status was suspect. We were on our own, and clueless!

Suddenly a lone cyclist was spotted paddling up the runway. The young Air Force officer greeted us with "Thank God you have come. We narrowly escaped a take-over last night!" It was later reconstructed that some subverted elements of the base were co-opted to be on key guard-duties to enable the 'comrades' hiding outside the perimeter, to take over the armoury and bomb dump after midnight. Simultaneous take-over of Temple-Trees (PM's Residence), Radio Station and the Port was planned. This plot was providentially pre-empted - I shall skip details of how!

Defending Katunayake Air Base - 1971

We were housed in some vacant billets and a meeting with a shaken Base Commander arranged. He wanted me to secure the Air Force Base at the earliest. Beyond that there was a total blackout about the situation.

The perimeter of the Base stretched more than 15 kms and was surrounded by thick coconut groves. It so resembles the situation that arose at the Pathankot Air Base in Jan 2016- except for their lucky escape in 71!

I identified the most vulnerable areas, which could be protected with my resources. By next morning we were dug in and in control of the bomb-dump, armoury and aircraft parking areas. My mortars and MMGs were tactically deployed, and patrols were combing the gaps. That uplifted the morale within the Base and normal life started to creep back. Meanwhile, the few aircraft of the RCyAF and their Army were busy shooting up any suspicious movement. Ceylon (Sri Lanka) had been a 'pearl of peace' in the Indian Ocean ever since *Ramayana*. So a ruthless reaction to unprecedented violence was not unnatural, as subsequent history has also shown.

A flight of IAF helicopters arrived at the Base for operational sorties, as no road was secure. An Indian liaison team of three senior officers representing each Service were positioned in Colombo. They focussed on diplomatic and strategic aspects. I virtually remained on my own as a quick-response force for an emergency. I frequently flew to Colombo for meetings at the Embassy and with the Sri Lankan authorities.

A call on Mrs. Bandaranaike clarified her political sensitivities and deft balancing between power-blocks. Warlike stores arrived from all sides e.g. US and USSR. She was even-handed in requesting India and Pakistan for troops, but the latter sent only two helicopters (based in Colombo) as their hands were full in East Pakistan. A massive airlift of Pakistani forces was going on via Colombo as over-flights over Indian airspace were banned. PAK aircraft would park in the farthest corner for refueling-we maintained surveillance.

Sri Lankan PM, India's HC, Service
Chiefs, our LO's and Me.

Two warships of the Indian Navy patrolled the sea routes to interdict foreign support to insurgents. All these measures and the heavy-handed Sri Lankan response resulted in the situation slowly stabilising. We shifted gears to provide training support and upgrading of combat capability. I was flown to their Officers Academy in the hills, but no meaningful contribution can result from a flash visit.

I was happy that we were not involved in offensive operations. I could sense the deep public suspicion of the Big Brother's tiny toe-hold viz. small support spinning into a serious scenario! Indian bullets shedding Sri Lankan blood would be a replay of *Ramayana without a Ravana*- and fatal for the Sri Lankan Govt. Tamil sentiment at the time favoured our presence; but how the tables have turned since! Routine operational activity continued until end of May, followed by our de-induction by sea.

We were back in Bangalore by early June '71. We had done a decent job (without blood-letting) and earned all-round acclaim for our professionalism. Warm letters of commendation from all Sri Lankan Chiefs were not mere gestures of protocol. It was a gesture of exceptional grace for the Chief, Gen. Maneckshaw MC, to address a letter of appreciation directly to me - a precursor of the now celebrated COAS's Commendation!

Indo-Pakistan War

My stay in Bangalore was short-lived. My wife and friends had already started calling it my temporary-duty station. The war-clouds in the East were growing ominous. We were ordered to mobilise and families had to be sent home.

Despina asked me to talk to them before closing the Family Welfare Centre. I was honest with them "we are going for war and I cannot guarantee that no one will get hurt or worse. But I promise that whenever I send your men into danger I shall be with them." During this meeting a problem of a JCO's wife came to light. She had a history of miscarriages and was in an advanced stage of pregnancy. She could possibly not go home. Before I could respond, Despina offered to keep her in the CO's residence and take care of her through her delivery. She did so and there was a happy ending- a healthy boy and a happy mother were sent home after some months!

In July '71 we were on our way to our battle stations. My military-special train steamed into Pune and I saw another on the parallel track. It was a Unit of the Madras Regt. I walked across to meet their CO. Lt Col Alexander received me warmly and offered a drink. In a morbid twist of fate we met again, six months later. He was in a coffin and my battered body was on a stretcher with a drip and a Doctor, being air-evacuated to Pune. A sniper's bullet had killed him a day after the cease-fire, and I had blown up on an anti-tank mine two days earlier. That is destiny, by higher design!

Let me recapitulate relevant aspects of the Indo-Pak War of 1971. Its centre of gravity was in the East- now Bangla Desh. Therefore the order of priority for re-equipping and resource-allocation within our Army was Eastern Command- then Western and lastly the Southern Command units. We had to accept serious deficiencies and capability constraints, smilingly. In order to survive and succeed in battle we had to optimise use of local resources, colloqually called 'jugaad'!

The strategic aim on the Western and Southern Army fronts was 'offensive defence'. This was translated variously into 'intentions and objectives' for Units. But at Unit level a war is a 'once in a lifetime' opportunity to earn 'honour and glory' for the *Paltan* and the Regiment- the sector/strategic priorities are irrelevant! It is not easy to resolve the implications of this dissonance at Unit level, especially when comparing results and rewards later. In fact, we did succeed in penetrating to a depth of 50 KMs- yet remained the 'forgotten-front'; like FM Slim's Army on the Burma front, till 1944.

By mid-Nov '71 we had staged forward to Chotan (see map below) ending the suspense about our employment through Gujarat or Rajasthan. It was going to be Barmer sector of Rajasthan- Sindh border.

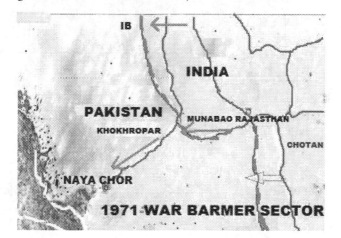

My 2IC (Walia) and QM (Attar) inspired the Sarpanch (village-head) of Chotan to be prepared to follow us across the Border with eight camels and handlers, for intimate logistic support. We had been training with their camels earlier-this was 'jugaad' at its best. These local Rajputs had cross–border connections but had not bargained for going 50 kms deep. The Sarpanch was awarded the Shaurya Chakra, a gallantry award, for services rendered, above and beyond any call, compulsion or compensation!

On 3/4 Dec. Pakistan Air Force launched pre-emptive strikes on our airbases and two bombs fell on Chotan. We were in our starting-blocks and ready to roll across the Border, with 85 Inf Bde leading through Munabao.

Initially, we were part of a special task-force, with the Engineer Regiment, to ensure restoration of road-rail link between Munabao and Khokhropar- the vital lifeline for operations including move of guns, ammunition and essential needs. We crossed the Border immediately after the leading elements.

Pushing Rcl Gun jeep in the desert - 1971

The task was accomplished despite frequent air attacks. We were the first Indian troops to enter Khokhropar, as the enemy had offered little resistance and the leading troops had bypassed it. We were tasked to secure it.

The Pakistan Air Force intensified interdiction attacks and the mines below started taking a toll. One of my trucks went up in flames and a rocket hit too close for comfort. Atma and I hit the dirt fast and for the first time I reached for my steel hat, suppressing the Cdo-bravado of combat in a soft hat – a WW 2 symbol of fearless defiance!

85 Bde continued the advance as they had not faced serious opposition till then. At this stage two things happened:-

(a) Brig Kataria, Commander 85 Brigade, blew up on a mine on the desert track ahead of Khokhropar. As per intelligence reports it should have been a gravel road- Pakistan had fooled us again! Our commander, Brig Gurjit Singh, was asked to take over that Bde.

(b) In the Jaisalmer Sector (see map) our flanking Division was poised to launch an offensive. But it was pre-empted by an enemy thrust against Longewala (see map) on night 3/4 Dec. The Pakistani commander had bragged that he will have lunch in Ramgarh and dinner at Jaisalmer. But within 16 kms of ingress our Air warriors and a company of 13 PUNJAB at Longewala had stopped the thrust and decimated all tanks and guns. By 7 Dec the remnants of the intruding force were in full retreat. The following extract from a 2012 blog titled 'Official History of 71 War' is relevant:-

BATTLE OF LONGEWALA

"Indian Army should have pursued and destroyed the enemy force (*but some commanders lacked initiative*).... The lessons of Longewal are clear: success in any endeavour requires balancing caution with courage. The Indian commander in the Jaisalmer sector lost out because he was too cautious while his Pakistani counterpart lost his job because he threw caution to the desert winds. And war can ... be brutally unforgiving..."

I have added this context to make a point about capability, courage and missed opportunities. By 7/8 Dec, enemy reserves in this sector were seriously depleted. The tide of war on both fronts was in our favour.

Our Div had managed to maintain momentum despite limited air cover, ground-friction and serious build-up constraints. Two conflicting issues arise:-

- Was this a time for caution or courage?

• What was the definition/limit of *'offensive-defence'* in this sector?

Since this is not a battle study, but my reflections, I shall leave these open-ended!

At this stage my Unit was coiled up, cohesive and itching for a fight. Much credit for this is owed to a highly spirited youngster, Lt Deswal. I had tasked him to ensure that all supporting echelons (which included two-wheel drive, non-sand-tyred vehicles) must keep up no matter what. He did that by employing creative improvisations like ad-hoc 'dhakka' parties. His go-getter spirit continues till now.

Our forces were making good gains but fitfully. With every passing day leading troops were moving beyond limit of our fire support, logistics and air cover. By 10/11 Dec stiff resistance was encountered at Parbat Ali- an advance position of enemy's main defences at the edge of the green belt.

I saw the Parbat Ali battle from close quarters as I was located nearby, being part of the Bde Orders Group (O Gp). The leading Bns had been under effective enemy fire for two days. It took that long to build-up adequate artillery support. The Inf Bns then mounted a gallant frontal assault through the minefields. It was a sheer 'blood and guts' bayonet battle and effective fire support that won them a 'bridge-head', on top of the dune.

At that stage Pakistani forces would have been dispirited. Dacca's fall was imminent and setbacks had been suffered at Longewala and Parbat Ali; in fact all along the western front. Was this the time for caution or courage? Should we exploit the break-in at Parbat Ali and/or threaten the other flank to sustain our momentum- I certainly felt so!

I was motivated by a passionate wish for my Unit to get a worthwhile opportunity- my Unit was readily available, willing and able. I should stage the Unit forward and be in 'starting-block status' to grab any opportunity. This was my thinking and the context on 14 Dec 71.

I met Brig Gurjit who had reverted to his own command. He indicated that the Brigade's task now was 'to capture enemy positions south of Parbat Ali'; and 2 GRENADIERS will carry out Phase 1 of the operation.

This was a warning order and a trigger for my actions. A reconnaissance (recce) from the southern flank (the most likely avenue of employment) was an imperative. I briefed my staff and tasked Walia and Nagpal suitably.

Walia drove me to follow in Nagpal's recce party. After a while he left and I took the wheel, to continue with the mission. I overtook Nagpal at about 1400 hrs as his Jeep had overheated due to cross country driving in soft sand.

Maj Atariwala, my Battery Commander (BC) was seated alongside, with Atma in-between to keep me orientated. I overtook the protection party vehicle which was struggling in the sand and asked them to cover us by fire. Atma spotted some footprints - no Indian troops had passed this way. I asked my Gunner adviser to keep guns on call in case we needed extrication. We had hardly gone a few hundred metres when there was a deafening bang and an indefinite blackout. I had managed to get blown up on an anti tank mine-one of the 75000 laid in front of enemy's defences, as per information shared by a Pak (Bengali) amputee in our hospital.

When I regained consciousness I realised that I was still in this world. My mangled body was upside–down, having been thrown up and out. A limb-count showed all present but frozen in-situ- nothing would move. The blast of the anti-tank mine had made the Jonga do a high-jump and twist, scattering us like peanuts. Groans indicated other survivors.

The blast was under my wheel so I was the worst-hit- my right foot was sheared at the ankle, right arm shattered, fragments embedded all over, and extensive burns up to the neck. Others had suffered fractures of various kinds; Atma had lost one of his eyes.

Luckily, Nagpal was close and Walia not too far away. The former arrived first, and retracing my tyre tracks, evacuated us one by one. For this gallant act he deserved the highest award but our award system is not perfect!

It took an hour to reach the Battalion HQ and two more till the cas-evac helicopter arrived. Atma and I were heli-lifted to the Triage-centre at Munabao. During this flight two enemy aircraft did some target practice on us, which our pilot evaded with clever nap-of-earth flying.

There was a long line of stretchers outside the underground operating bunker at Munabao. The surgeon walked down the line prioritising cases as per criticality, with the anesthetist following. The latter recognised me. He asked the Surgeon "You have not listed the Colonel for surgery" and was told that there was no pulse and the patient is not likely to survive surgery. "I know him; he is a survivor we cannot let him go" pleaded the good Doctor. "OK, put him on jet-stream blood plasma and I will review" said the other. I was told all this by both of them, many years later. After 16 bottles of plasma I was an acceptable risk for surgery.

After overnight lifesaving surgery including an amputation, I was heli-lifted to Jodhpur. Years later I went back there as the Desert Corps Commander! From 15 to 19 Dec. it was more surgery and a touch-and-go survival battle. Gen. Bewoor, the Army Commander, visited the battle-casualties and I asked him as to why aircraft could not be provided to evacuate critical cases. He was livid with the Comdt who had told me so. His reason was that some of us may not survive a long air evacuation.

Next day a pressurized aircraft was made available to take us to Pune. I preferred to go there as my brother-in-law was posted in AFMC and Despina would have family-support and a firm-base. She was desperate to see me alive!

Enroute to Pune the aircraft was diverted to pick up someone from Bhuj- it was Col Alexander in a sealed box! Two COs' wives, in a state of shock, and my sister were at the airport to receive us. After that it took nine months of multiple surgeries (including a second amputation and many reconstructive surgeries) for me to get a new life. My faith in the Military-medical system has not diminished since.

Seeing my state on arrival, Despina asked the Hospital priest to administer the 'last rites'... just in case? She would not like me to go without 'absolution' as per her tradition.

Many VIPs visited us, including the Prime Minister and the Defence Minister. I asked the latter about our retention in service. His reassuring reply was "Any war-casualty willing to stay will not be asked to go- we care for you all!"

My former GOC, Gen. Anand Mathur, who was then the Military Secretary came

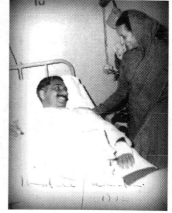

Pat from the Prime Minister-1972

to visit the casualties. He asked my wife "Where would you like to go next?" She reflexively responded- Bangalore! He pondered, looked at my shattered arm and said "Yogi, practice writing with your left hand, and the day you can write I shall post you near Bangalore." Some months later I wrote a letter to him and he posted me as Instructor at Staff College. He had met all officer-casualties and given everyone their choice posting!

One of the military institutions that remain unsung and under-recognised is the Military Nursing Service. These ministering-angels literally live up to the credo 'care for them better than their mothers'- they care, coax, complain even curse, just to heal. They turn into fuming furies (especially during Commandant's round) to keep their wards sparkling clean. Some patients were awkward, even aggressive, when in a state of delirium or intolerable pain. Some Nursing officers were coy others conventional- a few would be full of fragrance of sandalwood (after prayers); their touch always soothing. An OT sister had a special prayer-place in the operation-theatre; even the most disciplinarian surgeon would stand with head bowed till she finished her prayer before each operation. All doctors know that they treat but He heals!

Those nine months (Dec 71-Sep 72) were transformational- in a sense I was 'born again!' Much of the time I was bedridden due to two disabled right-side appendages. My wife and children and rest of the family kept me company during visiting hours. Despina had special permission to come during working hours for welfare visits. She would go to everyone in the ward to 'mother' them and then update me on each one's status. But that still left so many hours to keep staring at the ceiling and introspecting- it is my second nature now!

Some 'well-wishers' told my wife that I did not have to go so far forward! Surprisingly, Gen. Bewoor, the then Chief, casually remarked "We don't like to lose good CO's" when he met me in Staff College. The Commandant observed and asked me later, "your face went red; why?" I said "Sir, what kind of a signal does that send out- lead from a safe distance or that CO's should be in 'cotton-wool'? The only leadership I know is, "Follow Me!" He nodded and moved on.

Jammu 2014- Senior Sardars (veteran JCOs) of the 2nd Bn, with a younger Col Kotwal. Reunion with a former CO.

I have worn my game-leg with a sense of pride. I was right up-front, ahead of my troops and had kept faith with the high tradition of the CO's of the Second to None.

It was my privilege to lead a great Team in 1971. Sadly I have not acknowledged each one's contribution by name in this account. When I visited Jammu in 2014, all old Sardars (veteran JCOs) came to meet me from all corners of Himachal, Punjab and J&K- it was heartwarming!

While I am grateful for the award of the Vishisht Seva Medal (VSM) and prestigious posting as Instructor at the Defence Services Staff College and later College of Defence Management, my greatest reward is experiencing the love of my fellow Grenadiers and the sacrifices they have made; the undying love of my wife, Despina, and the family, and my personal transformation as a result of it. For that there is no substitute. I feel grateful for the opportunity to fulfill my 'dharma' in keeping with the spirit of the Chetwode credo. The mine-blast was a small price to pay!

CHAPTER 6

Till My Next Command- A New Trajectory

Contrary to conventional wisdom I did opt to stay on in service. Col Palsokar, MC, an elder Grinder who was the Director Resettlement at HQ Southern Command put lucrative resettlement options on the table. These included a petrol or cooking-gas agency at a place of choice or a management job with House of Tatas, State Bank of India and so on. I showed the list to Despina. She shared it with my sister. After some girly- giggling, she responded 'Let us take a petrol station; Santosh and I will shake our booties in mini-skirts while topping-up cars. That should attract customers'! I got the message, dripping as it was in syrupy sarcasm. I thanked the good Colonel and extricated myself with 'Sir, my posting as Instructor Staff College is a professional challenge that excites me. I may look at these options later'.

Did we (it was a joint decision) make the right choice? In hindsight, it has proved to be so! Many battle-casualties, similarly handicapped, chose to opt out. Financially, and in terms of creature comforts, they led a better life. But at a deeper level they did envy my flag car and starred status and most of all missed that 'something-special' of the life in uniform. In the ultimate analysis it is a matter of 'values' that one cherishes most! If the *kaal-chakra (wheel of life)* could take me back to the same cross-roads in life, my choice would be the same- and not because of the 'flag or stars'!

In effect, what I had lightly called an 'exciting-challenge' was a scary scenario! Staff College is the acme of military excellence. Its staff and students are the crème la crème of India's Defence forces. I was going to be the first ever Instructor with a 'game leg' amongst the finest group of gladiators in uniform. Some self-doubt was inevitable; but it also unleashed the animal instincts, the bull-dog spirit!

Before going south to the Nilgiris, we visited Jammu. My former commander of Nagaland days was commanding an operational Division nearby. He had won an MVC (second highest gallantry award) in 1971 and was a rising star in his own right. He rushed to meet me and was happy that I was not strapped to a wheel-chair or standing on crutches. He invited us to a lavish display of his hospitality and a war-victor's gung-ho life-style!

Within a year he was court-martialed for having fallen prey to temptations during the aftermath of the victory in Dacca. The Military can be ruthless in dealing with fatal flaws or moral turpitude! He was susceptible to temptations even in Nagaland, which had at times posed a moral dilemma (*dharma sankat*) for me as his Brigade Major. My response (to myself) was: 'I am not the keeper of my military senior's morals- his seniors are!' That was my view then and it remains so- otherwise the structure of military command would crumble!

By Sep 1972 we were on our way to Wellington in my new car. It was a special release out of Army Headquarters quota-- normal waiting time was two years. It was a thoughtful blessing from my former GOC, Gen Mathur. During his visit to Pune as the MS, he had seen my wife riding around on a scooter. He ensured that a car was released along-with my posting. The car was not modified for handicapped driving and I did not have a driver with me-my streak of madness was clearly not in the lost- leg!

Staff College is a tri-service Institution with a unique ethos. Its professional excellence is a legacy of its visionary founder, Maj Gen Lentaigne. He had selected this location and established the Staff College in the Nilgiris (literally 'blue-hills') after the partition of India- its earlier *avatar* is in Quetta, Pakistan.

I was appointed a Syndicate Directing Staff (DS)- which is the preferred term (instead of Instructors). DS are meant to direct students study and self-development, rather than teach them. The faculty's pecking order is not based on service-seniority but as per date of appointment as DS. I felt tickled at superseding (for protocol purposes at the College) even seniors who joined later. It included full Colonels posted-in directly as senior-instructors (SIs) as they had to first prove themselves as Syndicate DS. The purpose of this convention is to flag the 'primacy' of the DS in this Institution!

Another interesting innovation is the process of continuous evaluation and quality control. It involves two best and worst samples of student's work filtering up weekly through the Syndicate DS-Senior Instructor-Chief Instructor to the Commandant and back. At each level detailed comments are endorsed in a distinctive color ink. Performance-perception thus gained, about the DS and the students, is then corroborated on the ground. This is in addition to the formal assessment-system which earns M Sc (Defence Studies) degree from Madras University.

But there is a lot more to the Staff College than academics. It offers a fascinating blend of extra-curricular, sports and social life for officers and families as a part of overall development. Despina was in her elements during the SCADS events (Staff College Amateur Dramatics Society). She also started teaching French in the local Convent and Athena joined a prep-school quaintly named Holy Innocents- the military-brats studying there were anything but that! Many years later Arun attended the Staff Course and we spent a nostalgic week with him.

We went for boating/rowing to Ooty and Pykara lakes, trekking in Kotagiri hills and often drove downhill to Coimbatore for *dosas*. The term-breaks were family bonding time during road trips to back-waters of Kerala, Rock-memorial at Kanyakumari, Velankani shrine on East Coast etc. Despite the heavy load of preparation and correction work it was a blissful phase of life.

During my second year I was elevated to the Training Team as DS (operations). All the Team–mates of the time e.g. Vijay Madan and Guru Bakshi, rose to eminent three-star assignments. Training Team is the in-house think-tank, responsible for updating of exercises, war games and other instructional material. The daily briefings of the DS, dry runs/ conduct of outdoor exercises and writing conceptual papers are a part of the job-package. We also attended field exercises to keep in touch with ground realities.

During a war- game the new Comdt, Gen Smoky Malhotra, decided that some DS will play the role of commanding generals of Divisions- I was one such. It gave me quite a kick to dress up and act as a General. I did it rather well- neither sweat nor a note in hand (I was the author of the exercise). My orders drew special compliments from Naval and Air Force officers- one of whom Sushil Isaacs (later Chief of Naval Staff) said he had found a role-model that day!

I was permitted to pick a place at a lower height during mountain-warfare exercises. I declined saying 'I will start earlier but reach the top in time'! Thereafter, no concession was demanded or given- this was not to show off but to make a point that disability is in the mind more than the leg!

We were directed to upgrade instruction on 'disaster relief operations'. There was hardly any, except normal 'aid to civil authorities'. Someone mentioned that I had recently gone to Sri Lanka. It was assumed that it was for disaster-relief. The task of designing a new capsule fell in my lap. I assembled a study group and loaded it with foreign students- from US to Australia, and in-between- and challenged them to tap all their sources, and genius! Everyone stretched, including their ladies, in researching, writing, rehearsing and making a stunning presentation. It covered the full spectrum of disaster-relief operations from UN Disaster Relief Organisation to local administration. It was handsomely commended and many a request was received for a copy of the script-I was a satisfied catalyst!

But it was not always 'honey and roses'! During a classified sand model discussion (for Indian officers only) I was ripped apart by the visiting Vice Chief of the Army. He was specially critical of minefield planning 'the bloody mines were sprayed so liberally as if they were peanuts'. That was quite unfair as I had double-checked my calculations, with expert help of DS (Engineers).

Later the same General officer commended my confidence level and conduct of discussion, locally and in Delhi. I was getting congratulatory calls, while I was silently sulking. But the Comdt did something unprecedented. He directed the Chief Instructor to publicly announce that the Vice Chief had reconsidered and withdrawn his remarks. It was, indeed, an act of exceptional grace. I learnt later that the real target of the loose-cannon shots was the Comdt-I had just become collateral damage. So much for 'Games Generals Play'!

All this added up to my being rated amongst the top, even in that highly competitive group. It was not a sympathy-rating for a handicapped faculty member. The Comdt also took up strongly that despite my low-medical category I deserved to be nominated for Higher Command or Long Defence Management Course (LDMC). The normally bureaucratic MS system responded positively and I found my name in the select list for the year-long defence-management course at the College of Defence Management (CDM).

A Management Student and More

By the third quarter of 1974, I joined a formidable group of high-fliers from all three Defence (and some civil) Services for post-graduate level training at the Institute of Defence Management (now CDM). It was then the newest Joint-Services institute of higher learning which ran management training courses for three tiers of officers' viz. colonels, brigadiers and major generals. We were the fifth batch (LDMC-5) of its flagship course.

We were two 'psc daggers' (symbol of a former Staff College Instructor's pride); and both of us carried a cynical-chip on the shoulder about the new fangled management hot- air, mainly jargon! Ironically both of us ended up as faculty members and my elder colleague, later Vice Admiral RS Sharma, even became its Commandant.

After my family joined in Jan 75, we shifted into Rashtrapati Nilayam staff quarters. These are a part of President of India's southern estate and conveniently located in the Cantonment, within walking distance of the CDM Campus. We were comfortable and looked forward to a happy stay.

Athena got admission into the prestigious St Ann's Convent and Arun in St George's Grammar School, Hyderabad- he later shifted to the Central School in Secunderabad. Incidentally, these are twin-cities separated by a *tank-bund* (lake-side). We settled into a cosy routine of work, play and social life. Since then the romance of Secunderabad has crept up on us to the extent that we have chosen it as our final resting place. Once again, distant immigrants had turned natives- validating my thesis that 'history of mankind is a story of migrations and cultural re-mixes'!

The course tempo relaxed and we began to enjoy its cerebral-content. It offered new horizons of study including exposure to captains of industry and corporate management practices. It enabled cross-fertilisation of ideas and a study of parallel environments. The contrast from nuances of military leadership and culture revealed respective strengths and grey-areas. All this offered a rich opportunity for growth. The hard-core military hierarchy has, rather unfairly, treated management as an irrelevant intrusion and as a resettlement benefit. This is due to an insular and inbred military culture!

During the course I was made the leader of a Project study tasked to 'optimise logistics support system of a Mountain Division in Sikkim'. Col (later Maj Gen) Roy a batch-mate from IMA was our DS In-charge; and my NDA course-mate, KN (later Maj Gen) was de-facto deputy. Roy resented that we did not take him seriously- we just couldn't! He was from the technical graduates' course which was our junior for six months, graduated with us and then gained two years ante-date seniority. He could not forget some perceived- humiliations inflicted by us- two NDA striplings half his age- in his first term in IMA. His efforts to over-assert now seemed a travesty of natural order to us. Later in the 60s, all of us had also been Instructors at Faizabad. He had got married then and our wives had taught the new bride all the naughty-things of married life, being protocol-seniors! His pushing his tail now was a bit too much!

The study-team prepared a cracking report and our presentation was well received. That Study became a show-piece of CDM projects as it involved a live problem of an operational formation. The Commandant, who was an ace fighter pilot, desperately wanted a combat-experienced Infantry officer on the Faculty. He strongly pitched for my posting. No Infantry officer had secured instructor grade in as many management disciplines. As I was not due for any criteria appointment, it was expedient for Army HQ to post me as a Head of Department in CDM.

I completed an eventful and fulfilling three years as a member of faculty in 1978- am skipping details to avoid clutter! I was approved for my next promotion and also informed that my tenure in the next rank would be no more than a year, prior to my likely promotion as a Brigadier. An in- situ extension was offered till then, if acceptable to me and the College. It suited everyone and was cheerfully accepted. An extended tenure did enable continuity of our children's education and proved to be a turning point in many ways.

Athena could complete her High School and Junior College. She was elected as the Head Girl (students and staff choice) of St Ann's in her final year in school and the President of the junior college (12th standard) in St Francis. She was able to upgrade her piano qualifications from Trinity College, London. Our girl had transitioned into a PYT- with all assets and arrogance of a 'Pretty Young Teenager'! During this time we met Schrag's, an American Missionary family, being neighbours. They had dedicated 40 years of their life in service of the poor in this distant land. They have had a strong impact on the values of our children and have been like family elders ever since. Elders do matter in inculcation of values in children.

In 1976, Despina and Arun were able to go to Athens to attend her younger brother's marriage and take care of her ageing mother- sadly it was the last time that she could do so.

Meanwhile my Father's health had deteriorated seriously. Before I could reach home he had passed away. I had to leave Athena in Schrag's care, when I had to rush to Jammu.

Despina's Brothers Wedding : Athens -1976

Next year we compensated Athena with a few months stay with the family in Greece. It is important to stay connected with one's roots, on both sides! We also decided to send Arun as a boarder to Bangalore Military School to provide a better opportunity for all-round development and an exposure to military-like life. He did not think much of it then but the Old-Boys spirit of the 'Georgians' (Military Schools are the inheritors of erstwhile King George's School system) is still very strong.

Despina availed of our extended stay to earn a formal qualification as a french teacher from the Central Institute of Foreign Languages. She used it to good effect later in Dehra Dun.

Coincidence conspired to enable me to acquire a plot of land and build a modest home (with loans) near the prestigious Secunderabad Club! I shall skip the labour-pains involved in doing so, except to mention the benign role of a Regimental officer Lt Col R Yadava, who was instrumental in our settling down here.

When I look back on all this I wonder if all this was at all our plan or it happened as scripted elsewhere?

In 1979 I was posted as the Deputy Comdt and Chief Instructor of the Indian Military Academy in Dehra Dun. It was ironic that the ultimate-underdog cadet of his time was considered the right choice to be the top trainer at this premier Institution!

Some Reflections

These seven years (1972-79) were a rare opportunity for self-development. DSSC had equipped me with higher military leadership skills. The CDM exposure expanded the horizon further and deeper-into behaviour dynamics and optimisation techniques. A new value had been added to my professional repertoire.

I had realised that military minds tend to resist new ideas- human nature is the filter! We are excellent at absorbing and applying knowledge but rarely in creating new ideas. Concepts are global but applications have to be culture-specific. Even highly advanced powers, including the US, are still groping to find the right way to deal with the existing primitive and fundamentalist threats all over the world. This experience had stimulated me to think more creatively or laterally!

I headed for my new job with new expectations and enthusiasm and a head muddled with such ideas!

CHAPTER 7

Bumps And Bruises As A Brigadier

Deputy Commandant's Ceremonial Parade IMA-1979

I confess that my recall of Academy-days is 'bi-polar'! I am inclined to treat my cadet-time as forgettable and experience of pre-commission phase as more of an underdog than an under-officer.

My tenure as Deputy Commandant and Chief Instructor turned out to be nearly as traumatic! But that does not detract in any way from the greatness and glory of this hallowed Institution!

Indian Military Academy (IMA) is one of the finest cradles of military leadership. Since its inception in 1932, by Field Marshal Chetwode, it has developed strong traditions, a proud reputation and has produced a galaxy of distinguished military leaders. Its credo 'Service before Self' is the brightest beacon of the 'spirit of soldiering'.

Notwithstanding its strengths, no Institution can claim to be always perfect in every-way. There is an ongoing need for improvement and renewal. Some of the experiences in this narrative need to be viewed in that context.

Life is never a smooth ride. A bump at step-one of my higher command did not surprise me. It seems that whenever I take a double-jump, I trip and fall! I was almost detained from taking high-school finals due to double-jumps; this time the system set me up for embarrassment at the start-point!

Looking sharp on Parade

My posting to IMA had surprised me. It must have shocked the Commandant (Comdt). His then Deputy- a hard-boiled Haryanvi- was a willful leader who ran a tight-ship. He had tamed (read terrified) everyone to submit to 'his will'. This was his third tenure as a Brigadier, after command of a Brigade and a key staff appointment. He had formally represented against policies of the (present and previous) Commandants as he did not like some of their policies.

Dy Comdt Salutes- the tilted palm is legacy of wounds of glory

A raw, one-legged, new promotee as his relief must have been seen as a steep fall in experience and maturity levels- an unwelcome prospect from the Commandant's comfort-zone. He suggested to the Military Secretary that the 'new-kid' be attached as under-study for a few weeks.

Consequently, for three weeks I went around the IMA, as Deputy Comdt-designate, wearing a Lt Col's badges. I diligently saluted all full Colonels with a twisted smile and a wicked thought about the role-reversal a month later! Some may see humour in this farce but I felt like the hero of a Greek tragedy, with a bruised ego! Mercifully, my family was not in station. Despina had stayed back to complete construction of the house at Secunderabad.

The Commandant's counsel to me after I assumed my appointment was, 'Be tough as nails like your predecessor, and play down your professorial persona'! Long ago he had dropped his intellectual- surname and was projecting the same complex on me. I found that to be rather condescending- he hardly knew me. In fact, I had been labeled a martinet-someone who expects and extracts very demanding standards- twice in my command reports- soft persona, my toe!

The Commandant was a good and honourable man, a high-calibre professional and a noble soul. He had successfully commanded a Bde in war, and attended a two year Staff course in Canada- hence highly ambitious! He also wore a menacing moustache to project a ferocious-image. Having missed his third 'star' in the first look, he was hopeful of a favourable review- provided all went well in this high-profile job. A 'namby-pamby' Deputy could not be allowed to screw that up!

In contrast, I believed that a leader who has to project a 'put-on persona' is not authentic and generally not trusted! Little did I realise that such 'value-divergence' can distract from harmony at higher levels! As it turned out, it did 'queer my pitch' a bit. This has been recurring experience in my life; which prompted my Daughter to ask recently 'Daddy, did you always have trouble with your seniors?' I knew that no man is a hero to his wife- but not even the children: 'Et tu brute'!

I had carried a hang-over of management ideas from my last assignment- so I tried to do a SWOT analysis here! The training and administrative systems at the IMA had matured at the 'best-practice' level, for existing needs. But I thought that young leaders should be prepared for tomorrow's battle-field - not yesterday or today's needs! The military is a living and dynamic system, it must renew itself constantly!

I did find the calibre of Instructors to be outstanding- this was a great strength. But there was a flip-side to it. They knew that they were the 'best' and that made many of them highly career-conscious and competitive. Ambition is a legitimate aspiration but when it becomes obsessive about outstanding grades, staff-college competitions and foreign selections, it could distract from the much needed 'missionary- zeal' and commitment.

Sadly, a rat-race had trickled down even amongst the gladiators of the corps of cadets, as illustrated here. One of the Senior-Under-Officers, who was a gold-medal prospect, was brought to me as a repeat absentee from Academy team practices. His candid response was 'Sir, Academy team practices clash with my Company (Coy) level competitions. I represent my Coy in multiple games which fetches me more than 20 merit points, while playing in the Academy team earns only 10. I have to improve my merit-ranking and medal prospects'! This was smart calculus by an ex NDA gold-medalist! But it made a mockery of our credo of 'Service before Self'! Had we seeded selfish careerism by over-quantification of our systems? That is ominous for the military ethos!

Even the trainers had become more concerned with 'grooming the gladiators' than uplifting the mass and mentoring the weak. The latter tended to be satisfied with 'survival-standards'. The award-winners were the trophy-showpieces, not the silent majority which was taken for granted!

This was my way of searching for the 'key result areas' (KRAs), which were emerging as:-

- To train mentally agile and thinking leaders rather than robotic/ over- regimented types.

- Re-adjust focus of mentoring from gladiators to 'silent majority".

- Reinforce 'Service before Self' spirit.

This was a challenging wish-list. In order to make a meaningful dent I would need full support from my seniors and staff. In hindsight, these KRAs remained elusive, for various reasons- some of which may be visible later. But it was not for want of trying!

We had started with small steps. The Training Team was reinforced with creative talent to catalyse change. Two outstanding officers- Maj (later Lt Gen) Hardev Lidder of Paras and Capt (later Maj Gen) GD Bakshi, GR were re-deployed as a think-tank. They did a splendid job in making training more realistic and interactive with case-studies, battle-illustrations, more realistic outdoor exercises and so on.

The existing 'interview-system' was made more intensive for effective mentoring. This did put an extra burden on the young Instructors and intruded on their honeymoon time- many were newly-weds. One young wife, who was the Comdt's niece, put it in his ear, in all innocence.

I was promptly directed not to put too much pressure on young Instructors! Such signals show trust-deficit and tend to be dampeners. A switch to a status-quo mode seemed to be a more prudent option. I was too inexperienced to dig in!

The ceremonial and socialising functions also needed full time commitment. The bi-annual Passing-out Parade (POP) is a celebrated-spectacle. The routine from rehearsals to reception and dispersal is like organising a daughter's marriage (without an event manager)- in fact, two of them every six months.

The commissioning ceremonies are attended by invitees from foreign Embassies, Parents and other guests. The routines and responsibilities are exhausting; but the satisfaction at seeing the finished product march across the Final-Step was always an emotional high. Few can resist a lump in the throat and a wet eye when listening to the haunting notes of Auld Lang Syne and watching the new 'young officers' slow march into the hallowed portals of Chetwode building!

**Gen Krishna Rao,
Commandant & self at
some Ceremonials - 1980**

The sports, extra-curricular and social calendars of each term were fully loaded with adventure and fun. The families were kept enjoyably engaged. All this was Despina's staple and she relished every bit of it; as much as I grudgingly bore it!

Guests and Dy Comdt's family

Athena became an indispensable star of end of term plays, even after I was posted out. At her age she was bound to attract attention, as eye-candy of hordes of starved young males on the campus! My son had rejoined us from Bangalore Military School. He was able to enjoy the incredible IMA facilities. Despina was much in demand as a french teacher- she was gainfully engaged by the Doon School, Cambrian Hall etc. Her multi-lingual skills enabled her to interact with foreign dignitaries, as seen in these photographs. Her equation with the Comdt's wife, all officers and families was enviably warm - despite her 'tiger mom' persona at home and as the driving-spirit of family welfare and ladies club activities!

It was by chance that the IAS Academy at Mussoorie decided to invite the Dy Comdt of IMA to conduct an orientation capsule for Probationers prior to their Army attachment. That cascaded into my becoming one of their regular guest speakers and Seminar panelists, on military matters. It led to mutually beneficial interactions between the two Academies.

Another extra commitment came my way in the form of a High Level Study Group on 'officers' career-management'. It was headed by Lt Gen Hira, MVC, General officer Commanding-in Chief, and comprised a hand-picked team of senior officers representing all Arms. I was the junior-most member- perhaps picked on the strength of my combat-experience and management qualifications?

We submitted a seminal report after six months of very intensive study. It was accepted for implementation by the then Chief. But it generated partisan controversy between the Pro-Infantry lobby and the Rest. This was owing to mis-information about our recommendations impinging adversely on promotion prospects of Infantry officers. Sadly, such tribal rivalries and turf-wars have been and will remain the bane of the Services!

My Commandant was aligned with the pro-Infantry lobby. I was now in a double dog-house in his eyes! He had suspected that my external-excursions were manipulated by me and now I was also tagged as an anti-Infantry agent? The default-position of many senior officers is 'distrust and doubt'- an anti-thesis of core values. Such things made my resolve to consolidate the Chetwodian credo seem like a pipe-dream.

Another lesson I learnt from this tenure was that troubles don't come alone. Let me share some incidents to prove this point.

Incident 1

Two days before commissioning of June 1980 course, a worried Bn Cdr reported a scandalous case of a Passing out GC who had made his local girl-friend pregnant, on promise of marriage. Her family was sitting in '*dharna*' outside his office.

The case compelled urgent action and instant disposal. Its consequences could be catastrophic. I left that GC with just one option 'get married now or be withdrawn'. Normally withdrawal requires Ministry of Defence approval, but nobody called my bluff. All parties saw sense. While his course-mates were Passing- out, he was getting married under supervision of his Coy Cdr. We had managed to keep the media hawks off our back.

Incident 2

A few weeks later a former NDA first-termer went berserk. This smart Sardar from Patiala changed his Sikh identity, without proper permission. After a drunken orgy in town he came back at midnight, in a disorderly state. He was locked up. After some days he again defied authority and was marched up before me. He declared that he could no longer tolerate military discipline. I was stunned- how had he developed this allergy after three years training in NDA? I referred his case for psychiatric review at the military hospital. They bounced him back after a few weeks with the opinion 'No psychiatric disorder detected'! The 'mad-sardar' was making a mockery of the system, to barely concealed bemusement of the cadet community. The Commandant expected me to deal with the problem as the Chief Instructor. I consulted Army HQ who advised 'due process'; and indicated that the Ministry may consider voluntary-withdrawal on refund of training costs? The GCs response was' my father cannot afford to pay anything; that is why he sent me to NDA to get a free degree. I have done that; now I want 'out'!

The penny finally dropped- all this was a pre-meditated drama, consummated by a cunning con-artist! I made him an ally- provided he agreed to be safely deposited at home, under escort. That was done. A case was prepared for 'Emergency Withdrawal of an Undesirable cadet', whose retention would seriously harm discipline and credibility of the Academy- for ex-post facto sanction of the Govt. The issue of 'reimbursement of costs', we suggested, may be resolved between initial contracting parties. This time it blew-over, but next time it blew-up, in my face!

Incident 3

This time one of the chronic defaulters fired a blank round at a senior cadet appointment from a dangerously close range. He had harboured a long-time grudge against him. It was a serious infringement and I was keen to send a strong signal to deter such behaviour. The defaulter had already collected 56 days restrictions for repeat offences – a total of 63 would invoke automatic relegation by six months. I recommended 'relegation' as punishment for this offence- the Commandant approved.

When I formally pronounced the punishment the guilty GC froze, in situ. He was physically removed and locked-up in the Quarter guard.

After a few hours the Adjutant recommended his release as he was showing remorse.

I had barely reached home for lunch when the Bn Cdr, Col Santokh Singh reported that the same GC had a loaded rifle and was calling for the Deputy Commandant and the Senior Cadet. Santokh advised me not to go as they were handling the situation. But I chose to go!

He was holding the rifle under his chin and acting as if 'drugged'- not an unknown phenomenon amongst an aberrant few! All efforts to convince and cajole him were having no effect. Various efforts were afoot to disarm him by surprise.

His Company commander, Maj Satbir Singh, was trying to get closer to make a grab for the gun. Suddenly, a shot rang-out and his body slumped. He was rushed to Hospital but did not survive. His father a retired JCO refused to come for the cremation! Loss of a young life is always deeply saddening- but I was not burdened by any guilt. I had done my '*dharma*' as per my light.

The aftermath of such incidents is ugly- small minds gloat, implicate and stigmatise. The media speculation went into overdrive, fed by malignant insiders. All that is par for the course, but the silence and vicarious insinuations of those who should have understood is hurting. The due process of investigation of the incident, including the Court of Inquiry by Col (later Army Chief) Padmanabhan, absolved me of any wrongdoing or responsibility for this suicide.

All along I had sheltered my family from my work-pressures. Despina had enough on her plate in dealing with two adolescent children. Now they stood by me like a rock and we lived our life as normally as possible. Innocently, my son asked me one day 'Dad, are you going to be fired?' I said 'I don't think so but it is not my call- all depends on higher authorities? But why do you ask?' He said 'Some GCs were saying that you are a good man but this will kill your career'. I shrugged!

A feverish frenzy of visits followed, including the Vice Chief's. He surprised a harassed newcomer with 'how do you feel?' The reflexive reply was 'like a rat!' I almost laughed and the Commandant glared, as if I should have coached him better. The Vice raved about his days when cadets were relaxed and allowed to drink beer over week-ends. I almost asked 'If we should also arrange nautch- girls!' He clearly did not know about adventures of the debauched-stud and the druggie, as recounted above!

My Commandant rewarded me with two mediocre reports. I used to treat my reports with contempt, being someone's opinion of my worth- not my self-worth in my own eyes! But a well-wisher insisted that I must represent on grounds of prejudiced-assessment. He even prepared a draft for me. And thus I submitted a statutory appeal for redress, which was substantially granted.

I draw satisfaction from the fact that not one of my subordinates felt any extra heat or suffered a scratch as a consequence of this incident. All of them got promoted and many reached very high ranks, including one Chief. I too survived!

Meanwhile, I started to re-explore job prospects outside. An open offer had existed since my CDM days. I was invited to meet the Board of Directors in Bombay and a visit was arranged to the production plant at Thane. They agreed to take me on board as No 2 as a part of a succession plan. I gave a conditional acceptance as there was still a remote chance of getting command of a Bde. In a corner of my psyche I was not comfortable with the business of money-making- it was not in my genes!

I limped along for a few months. The Commandant was posted out first. I worked with the new Comdt, Gen M Thomas for a few months. In early 1981 I was posted as Director Management Studies at Army HQ to replace Brig BC Khanduri (later Member of Parliament and a Central Minister). Were the Comdt and I both bowler-hatted? Perhaps! In our own way, we both had done our duty as best as we knew.

I drove my family into separated family quarters straight after my dining-out from IMA Mess. The family stayed there for next five years of my nomadic tenures. It enabled Athena to complete her Masters and B Ed; and Arun joined NDA. My children are justified in blaming me for being a 'remote father' during those crucial growing up years. Despina deserved a medal for filling in for both of us- it was not painless for her but she was a true-blooded trooper!

Army Headquarters- my First Foray

My new job was exciting, in as much as it was not a soul-destroying file-pushing assignment. It was the in-house consultancy directorate of General Staff Branch, under the Director Staff Duties (DSD) and Deputy Chief of the Army Staff, Lt Gen Sundarji.

Army Headquarters was virgin territory for me. I entered it with some diffidence and a streak of defiance. My Directorate was located on the 9th floor of Sena Bhavan (SB) and my immediate superior, Maj Gen MC Gupta, DSD, was located on Level 2 (=3 standard floors) of the majestic South Block. His typical fetish was to hold at least two grill-meetings every day- the second anytime between 6-9 PM. The General was a confirmed bachelor and a reputed 'sadist'. He was also sweating for his third star like my former boss (both were course-mates)! Was I lucky or what?

I soon discovered that I had to cope with a super-efficient control-freak. He was a Sapper officer (Engineers) who had commanded an Infantry Division. His command was distinguished by his Provost Officer threatening to jump into the Brahmaputra while hanging from a bridge. In my mental state such a Boss was perfect- for release of pent-up emotions.

I set myself a cracking routine. I would walk 5 kms from the Officers Mess to Sena Bhavan, climb nine flights of steps to my Directorate; wash up, change into uniform and be in my chair at 9AM sharp. I was informed by my staff officer (an EME Lt Col) that in Army HQ the Civilian Staff is incorrigible- they come whenever they feel like, half are running side-businesses and take leave of absence at will. For next three days I personally monitored attendance and sealed the register at 0930 hrs sharp- latecomers were docketed half/full- day pay as per rules. After one week the same staff became more regular than my combatant staff. Later the same lot would willingly work with us till midnight, when needed. Their meals and transport arrangements were made by us, out of our pockets if necessary.

There were four Study Teams under my command- each one handling three live projects at a time. Each Team was led by a Colonel General Staff and had a balanced mix of Service and civilian staff. The projects were approved at Deputy Chief's level based on a rigorous annual selection cycle at my level. I had to report daily progress to my boss during his morning roll-call. My charter included interim and final presentations, submission of final report and monitoring implementation on decisions taken. We could meet anyone, call conferences and travel anywhere for data collection and analysis. It was stimulating work.

A showdown was expected and it came within a few weeks. During a review meeting Gen Gupta was critical of my priorities. I was not devoting as much time as my predecessor to some of his favourite studies e.g. rationalisation of office accommodation in Army HQ. In my view it had no conceptual content and I had an excellent Colonel (former CDM colleague) doing a competent job.

After the conference I marched into his office, declined his offer to sit and made a formal submission 'Sir, you are not satisfied with my work. I am therefore requesting for a posting out, anywhere. I did not ask for this job and am prepared to move forthwith. ' He ordered me to sit down, take my cap-off and offered a cup of tea. He expressed full confidence in me and clarified that he had only made a comparative comment. My response was that I am accountable for 12 studies- hence the discretion to guide and supervise selectively should be left to my judgment, not imposed or judged by precedent. He agreed. When I was posted out he gave me the finest report of my career and spoke so warmly at my farewell that many commented 'kya jadoo kia re (what magic did you do?)'

After assessing our potential Gen Sundarji stretched us with some challenging studies related to functional effectiveness of Army Headquarters. A sample is given below.

> **Perspective Planning**. This function, per se, was nobody's baby then. We had to conceptualise the structure, system and process of preparing long term (20 years) Perspective Plans for the Army. The Directorate is fully functional now and meeting a vital need.

> **Equipment Management.** A new Equipment Management Directorate was created in the Master General of Ordnance Branch to fill an existing void. It is responsible for coordinated and result-oriented equipment management in the Army. It is taken for granted now but no such mechanism existed then.

His Military Assistant, Arjun Ray (later Lt Gen) mentioned to the Deputy Chief that I was looking outside for a job, if not given command. In our next meeting Gen Sundarji asked 'why do you want to command a Bde, to punch-ticket for promotion.' That term had gained currency during Vietnam War to refer to short command-tenures as passports for advancement. I replied' Sir, I joined the Infantry to command; not to push files for the next 15 years of my service'. He empathised and promised his support.

Within a few months he delivered on his word! I am told that he lobbied in my favour with the Chief, Gen Krishna Rao and the Army Commanders. Meanwhile brave-hearts like Cols Ian Cardozo (later Maj Gen) and Vijay Oberoi (later Lt Gen –C in C) had creditably commanded Units despite game legs. Ian and I received orders to command Brigades around the same time. I was posted to a Mountain Brigade engaged in counter-insurgency operations in Manipur on our Eastern-most border. And thereby starts the next saga of my story.

CHAPTER 8

Operational Command And Staff

THOUBAL Hill- my Bde HQ in Manipur. Plaque
shows history of NONGPOKCHING.

Prior to taking-over the Brigade, I went home to celebrate with the family. The breaking-news on TV came as a dampener: 'Military convoy ambushed on Road Imphal-Ukhrul'. 21 soldiers of a SIKH Bn killed as retribution for alleged gang-rapes', said the news. The females in my family were livid. 'How can our Jawans do such beastly things?' They did not know that propaganda is a weapon of the insurgents; and our media (and masses) are so gullible! I chose not to defend, without facts. But this incident gave them an insight into the challenges of my new job.

In case sending me to command a Mtn Bde in a remote hot-spot was the system's (military bureaucracy's) 'pound of flesh', it was a serious miscalculation. They had actually done me a favour. Counter-insurgency was my strong-suit by virtue of specialised training in the US and tenure in

Nagaland. The belief that a bureaucracy (military or civil) is *impersonal, unbiased and egoless* is a myth!

My fascination for the tribal culture and unique character of the North-East was deep-rooted- perhaps due to my *'pahari-pathan'*(North-western) extraction! The opportunity to command a Brigade (Bde) in Manipur was thus a gift.

181 Mtn Bde had been newly inducted from a peace station to deal with a growing nexus between Meitei Extremists in the Imphal Valley and Naga Hostile groups in the surrounding hill areas. Our inimical neighbours, China and Pakistan, were covertly fishing in troubled waters.

My Headquarters was located at Thoubal, South of Imphal on Imphal-Moreh Road. The Bde was responsible for operations in southern Manipur extending up to Myanmar and Mizoram borders. Two other Brigades were deployed to cover the Northern and Eastern parts of the State. Assam Rifles and Border Security Force (BSF) Units were responsible for border management and other security functions. It was a formidable force level to deal with a few thousand insurgents. It is this asymmetry that makes sub-conventional conflict e.g. insurgency/extremism/terrorism, such a malignant form of low cost- high return threat!

At the time, there were multiple extremist groups viz. the Vaishnavite Meitei- extremists in the Valley and various tribal groups on the surrounding hills. These included Nagas (North East and North West of Imphal) and Kukis, Hmars and Mizos (from South West of Imphal). Various alliances were being forged, internally and extra-territorially. The situation is even messier now in that sensitive part of our land!

Each group was fired by a spirit of sub-nationalism, identity-conflict or perceived grievances/deprivations of one kind or another. It was, and is never, a simple law and order scenario. The ineptness and corruption of the self-serving political and administrative class had added fuel to the fire. Inimical powers did, and will continue to, provide the oxygen and material support to keep the embers ignited-such is the nature of 'power-game' that nations play in the name of real-politik!

In the 80s the problem had gone beyond the control of civil administration- it is still bad! It had then resulted in an incremental involvement of the Army. But after induction of military force, all others tend to go into a spectator-mode i.e. compartmentalised working, turf-battles and a disjointed response. The District administration had become introverted and Imphal-centric. Remote areas were left to manage on their own or were at God's mercy and under insurgent control.

I informally shared these perceptions with His Excellency, the Governor (a former Home Secretary) and anyone else who mattered. I realised, for the first time, the reality of 'limitation of power' of even those considered powerful in matters of state.

The imperative of coordinated response was our greatest challenge. It needed out- of- box solutions, extraordinary skill and tact. Other stakeholders mostly thought otherwise. Military commanders are also more comfortable with robust Rambo-style interventions!

We were dealing with a shadowy and elusive opponent viz. misguided and unidentifiable 'sons of soil' operating on home-turf. We were the 'outsiders', at best or considered an 'occupation-force'. The metaphor of 'misguided fish swimming in a huge pond' is apt but its implications are rarely recognised. You cannot catch fish by watching it from outside; and if you wade-in, it is impossible to identify the 'misguided'. In the process, the toxic-types can sting seriously, as in that ambush. Then the reflexive response is to thrash-around furiously. Such strenuous exertions lead nowhere and the bad-guys keep laughing from their homes or hideouts. Frustrating? It is; but that is the nature of the beast called counter-insurgency or anti terrorist operations!

All this was happening when I arrived. After that ambush, frantic jungle-bashing was in progress and it went on for weeks. Everyone knows that no self-respecting insurgent hangs around in close or far vicinity of the incident site! But when no better option exists something has to be done.

On assuming command I sensed signs of a risk-averse culture! During our trip to Imphal, for dining-in and out ritual, our vehicle displayed no flag or star-plate. That was the existing policy- incognito Cdr! I found that intriguing, but it did not take long for the 'penny to drop'. The Brigade had recently hit the bull's eye in which a top extremist leader was captured. It was a bold operation by 17 JAK Rif in which Lt. (later Maj Gen) Pithawala had won the highest peacetime gallantry award. To sully the book now by exposing two cdrs to some hothead's potshots made no sense. Next morning, there would be screaming headlines: 'Two Indian Brigadiers ambushed'! Such publicity is oxygen for the extremists and a humiliation for Security Forces.

But such caution was contrary to my value system. Our soldiers follow their leader's example. I had seen it in war and experienced it in Nagaland. My first commander was a veteran of WW2 and 1962 conflict. His battalion had suffered heavy casualties which had made him risk-averse. That attitude had trickled downstream! His successor was a daredevil who had set the Bde on fire. Later they were the first to enter Dacca in Dec 1971- the Cdr was awarded the MVC. I had chosen my role model then. So up went the Commander's flag and star plates, and down came all barriers to civilian-military interactions (except undesirable fraternisation)! We could not sit on the banks of the big pond and hunt the bad fish!

Since the de-capping of the People's Liberation Army of Manipur (mentioned above), the centre of gravity of operations had become Valley-centric at the expense of outlying areas. That was the prevailing operational concept and deployment policy of the Division. Maj. Gen. Tubby Nayar, SM was the GOC of this oversized Division (more than fifty major units compared to fifteen of a standard division). He was responsible for operations in Nagaland and Manipur and came directly under HQ Eastern Command.

I had known him from our days in Wellington, where he was a Senior Instructor. We used to have heated professional exchanges then. These were destined to continue over two more of my tenures. This time our

94

perceptions differed on the concept of high and low-intensity areas and valley fixation. My case was that voids in the so-called low intensity areas (outside the Valley) left corridors for trans-border movement. Most of these were through my Sector.

But he was the boss, and his thrust was on breaking the 'back' of the largest Meitei group in the Valley. The GOC's strategy paid off when the Imphal Brigade trapped and killed another top PLA leader in an urban hideout, based on specific intelligence. The intrepid Bde Cdr, Som Jhingon, was awarded the Kirti Chakra for gallantry and was later nominated for the NDC course.

But insurgents are a hydra-headed monster- you cut-off one head, and another grows! Same is applicable to 'breaking the insurgent back'- it is so elastic that it bounces back! Within a few months, my view was also vindicated when a PLA gang exfiltrated to Burma through the outlying areas to join hands with Naga Hostiles (Muivah group) and get a massive resupply of arms from China!

Two brand new graduates from Staff College were posted as my principal staff officers- Major Davindar Grewal, Armoured Corps was the Brigade Major and Karnail Bhoon of EME the DQ (logistics chief). The good news was that both were totally innocent about counter-insurgency operations! They would be awe-struck by heated exchange between me and the GOC in the Operations Room and dumb-struck at the bonhomie over drinks in the Mess! The myth that expressing dissent to a higher commander was a 'kiss of death' stood busted for them forever after.

Despite being raw on the job, they did me proud with their sincerity, dedication and superb staff support. The BM and DQ rose to be Brigadiers. Karnail, who has one of the sharpest intellects, has excelled in the outside world also. The rest of the staff team was also highly motivated.

A number of Units served on my order-of battle (orbat) during this period. My experience fully validated Field Marshal Slim's observation that 'there are no good or bad units, only good or bad officers'. I was fortunate not to find any bad officers- only a few naughty ones- though some were brighter than the others. All Commanding Officers and Subedar Majors were awarded Vishisht Seva Medal (VSM). This was as mandated by the Army Commander (later Chief) Gen Vaidya, MVC **. Many other awards were won by all Ranks.

My Regimental elder Maj Gen (later Lt Gen) Yogi Tomar, who was commanding the flanking Division in Mizoram, visited my Bde Sector. He paid us a big compliment when he commented 'Yogi, everyone looks so cheerful and relaxed in your Brigade'. In contrast his policy of not shaking hands with the CO or not having tea in the Unit till they had captured/killed a certain number of insurgents had piled more stress on them. Negative incentives rarely add value, only tension. Our Units are driven by Regimental Izzat to do their best- if that is recognised and they are given support and freedom to excel, they deliver their best. That was my command philosophy and it has worked.

Two significant things happened midway during second year of my command. Maj Gen VK Sood, another colleague from Staff College days, was posted in as GOC and I learnt that I may be laterally shifted to take over the Imphal Brigade, as Som Jhingon had been selected for the National Defence College course.

My present HQ and one Bn were being redeployed in Mizoram. I sent a 'personal for' signal to the Chief, short-circuiting proper channels, protesting against the proposed lateral shift. Gen VK informed the Army Commander and suggested that he may wish to persuade an adamant Bde Cdr who refuses to be side-stepped. The Army Commander came and disarmed me with some cool logic 'Two thirds of your Bde is staying back and will be merged with your new Bde. Continuity in Manipur is an imperative and you are the right man to continue with the good work here'. I relented, apologized for breaking protocol and expressed faith in the judgment of higher commanders.

I have chosen not to burden you with trivia of tactics or operational details. The regrouping of the Sectors was carried out smoothly. Sustained momentum of operations to inflict attrition on insurgents was maintained. Actionable intelligence is the key and we had cultivated our own sources for that. It takes time, special skills and luck. Sources are personal, temperamental and work on mutual trust. One has to pamper, protect and reward them suitably. I even risked covert deployment of some assets, for trans-border intelligence.

We built bridges of trust and communication with civil administration and other agencies. I would update the Governor (Raj Bhavan was next door) on overall operational situation and my hassles with civil administration, if any. But our highest priority was on gaining public confidence, especially the youth and women-power (Nupi Lam). A special room was designated for anyone to meet me or my staff. No one was denied an opportunity to unburden their grievances. The empathy and a responsive attitude went a long way in establishing our good faith. My staff acted as a clearing-house for problems falling outside our domain.

I must acknowledge the invaluable contribution made by Maj KC Sharma, Arty who was posted as the Defence PRO. His media-management was incredibly effective and a force-multiplier for us. He would maintain a real-time scan of the situation in Nagaland, Manipur and the neighbouring States; and invariably take pre-emptive action before any negative-PR fallout happened. His networking and personal equation with national and local media ensured a fair-projection of our viewpoint. We learnt that it is best not to manipulate the media or fudge a message. It paid dividends then, and later in my career.

There were no big-bang actions during this period. I have never believed that we were in showbiz nor have felt the need to play to the gallery. We kept chipping away at the problem, which is as good a way of resolving it- that is the 'homeopathic-way' rather than radical surgery. Some of my operations did not succeed or met with partial success. We accepted those, learnt lessons and moved on; no zero-error syndrome in my command! I trusted the lower and higher commanders and they reciprocated. Gen VK Sood's command style was so enabling that it spurred one to keep doing one's best. Later he was also my Corps Cdr and remained a dear friend as the Vice Chief of Army Staff.

Suddenly I was warned to be ready to move at short notice for a special assignment at Army HQ. The situation in Manipur had stabilised sufficiently to allow short visits by families. I invited Despina and Athena to rush down, which they did; Arun was in NDA. Their visit to this exotic part of our country was memorable. My posting order arrived while they were still in Imphal. They were thus able to attend many an emotional farewell organised by the Army, Civil agencies and the locals.

The final farewell by groups of locals, including women and youth groups representing all segments in my Sector was heartwarming. They saw us off right up to the aircraft – even the Airport management and security staff played ball. It was a deeply emotional experience for us as it was essentially spontaneous- as if one of their own was leaving. I had expressly forbidden any stage-managed *tamasha*.

When anyone asks as to which was my most rewarding command- it was this; as the real reward came from those whose kin we had relentlessly hunted! The credit entirely goes to those who implemented my command directions. We did not resolve the insurgency in Manipur -it cannot be done by military operations only. But we did lower its threshold to restore normal life and uplifted the trust-level and the sense of belonging; they accepted us as their own. That was an achievement I am more proud of than any medal or other recognition.

Thank you all! We love you too.

I was awarded the ATI VISHISHT SEVA Medal for this command-extracts from the citation are illustrative:-

Investiture Ceremony

"ATI VISHISHT SEVA MEDAL

Brig Yoginder Nath Sharma took over command of 181 Mountain Brigade in an active counter-insurgency area in Mar 1982. As a result of his dynamic and determined exercise of command, his Brigade was able to effectively contain the Meitei and Mizo insurgent groups operating in Southern Manipur. They were thus unable to carry out any operation or establish any bases in his Brigade Sector, which had earlier been under extensive insurgent influence.

In May 1983, Brigadier Yoginder Nath Sharma took over command of 61 Mountain Brigade in the same area, covering an enlarged sector, which was earlier the responsibility of two Brigades. During the two months, since then, his Brigade has achieved striking successes. These include a major raid on an important NSCN hideout, and its follow up operations, which have seriously disrupted the infrastructure and the supporting base of the Naga undergrounds in the area. Another large scale search and destroy operation carried out against the PREPAK group led by its Self Styled C in C, has resulted in virtual decimation of this Meitei extremist group by the Security

Forces. The dreaded Terrorist Suicide Squad (TSS) was also disarmed during this period, when its leader surrendered to the Army, with four weapons, including one Sten gun.

With great effort he has also been able to restore the Civil-Military relations, which had come under some strain lately, to an even keel thus achieving a remarkable degree of cooperation and collaborative effort which is so essential for effective counter insurgency operations.

His vigorous leadership and meticulous planning have resulted in the capture of 36 extremists and recovery of one light machine gun, one Chinese automatic rifle, seven other rifles, one sten gun, six revolvers and large quantities of amns and explosives in less than two months.

Brigadier Yoginder Nath Sharma has thus rendered distinguished service of an exceptional order.

Rashtrapati Bhavan, New Delhi

31 Mar 1984"

(Extracted from the official book of citations distributed at the time of Investiture Ceremony at the Rashtrapati Bhavan)

A Creative Challenge at Army Headquarters

My new assignment in Army Headquarters stunned me! It was as No 2 of a special team selected to prepare the Army's case for the 4th Central Pay Commission. Money matters and I are mutually exclusive! The only entry on the monthly pay slip that I ever looked at was 'amount rendered to the bank'; which I found was never enough. My wife discovered it to her horror when she first visited the bank to check my credit balance. The Manager informed her that I was on permanent- overdraft except during first week of the month! Such was the culture and the military compensation-system of that time!

And now to be trusted with preparation of Army's pay case was the supreme irony! But when I saw the names of the Adjutant General, Lt

Gen K Balaram, PVSM and the Chairman- designate, Maj Gen Naresh Kumar, PVSM** it began to make sense. Both had been fellow members on the high powered Gen Hira Committee. Perhaps they had seen some sparks that I have not! Gen Naresh was promised by the Chief that he will be given his choice-team for this onerous assignment. He bid for me and Col (later Lt Gen) Kulbir Suri based on personal knowledge and left it to the MS to select the best available Colonels from other Arms and Services.

The Team had assembled by the time I joined. It was a well qualified group- Surjit from EME was an M Tech from IIT, Lalit Gupta of Engrs was B Tech and a distinguished combat engineer, Viren Bajaj of Signals, a B Tech in telecom-engineering and Lalit Ahuja an MBA. But none had any pay administration or accounts background, unlike our Air Force or Naval counterparts. But it was a highly motivated group of fast- learners.

We were an ad hoc organisation sanctioned for six months at a time. It was pointless to move my family to Delhi - they kept visiting regularly. Initially I stayed in the Mess, till moving in with my Brother in Law, Maj Gen Magotra, who was posted as the Deputy Comdt of the Army Hospital in Delhi Cantonment. Two staff cars were released and put on call for our exclusive use. This eliminated the normal irritants of an Army HQ posting and we were able to devote ourselves fully to this creative challenge.

We organised ourselves into three teams- to evolve new pay structures and other entitlements for officers, Other Ranks, allowances and pensionary benefits. Gen Naresh provided command guidance, conceptual inputs and took care of Inter-services matters and environment management.

Our work involved serious research, data collection and analysis, brainstorming sessions, presentations, Inter-service coordination, drafting and cycles of iterations till completion of the final report. Gen Naresh and I took turns to take the Pay Commission members to visit all types of field areas for a feel of the hazards and hardships of military service.

I believe that we projected a good case, which was vetted at all decision making levels up to the Chiefs of Staff Committee. All Pay Commission members were supportive of our cause. It is another matter that the Bureaucracy played foul at the implementation stage! It has taken years of litigation for final redressal of the 'rank pay' mischief. The inequities inflicted on the military pay and status equations, since 3rd Pay Commission to date, are a long litany, which is beyond the scope of this narrative.

After two extensions of six months we had completed our task to full satisfaction of the hierarchy and our own expectations. I was approved for promotion and was also able to attend the Investiture ceremony at the Rashtrapati Bhavan, along with my family. Athena got a chance to meet the charismatic Prime Minister, Mrs Indira Gandhi; but within months the PM was assassinated by one of her body guards, to avenge the operation to flush out armed Sikh militants from the Golden Temple.

Gen Naresh was selected to raise the National Security Guard where he earned a bar to his PVSM. This was one of the few No 2 jobs that I had fully enjoyed, mainly due to his exceptional human and leadership qualities. It was also a joy to work with an intellectual giant like the AG, Gen Balaram; and a great Team of bright officers. A few months later I got promoted and was posted to command a part of the Infantry School at Belgaum.

CHAPTER 9

Breaking The Glass Ceiling

When I assumed command of the Belgaum-based Junior Leaders (JL) Wing of The Infantry School, it was a historic 'first'. Never before had a physically-challenged officer reached a two-star General's rank in the Indian Army. Once this glass-ceiling was cracked, many physically 'challenged' officers rose to flag-ranks along that trail. It was due recognition of the resilience of our military leaders and the Army's enabling-ethos!

My Family - Infantry House Belgaum-1986

After a separation of nearly five years the family was together again. We knew that it would be a truncated tenure, till a vacancy arose for command of an Infantry Division, which was the criteria-command in that rank. We were inclined to look upon this tenure as an R&R break-quite unaware that a higher-purpose was 'scripted' in it! There have been many mind- boggling turning-points in my life to be called coincidences!

Belgaum is a World War II era military station at the cusp of the Western Ghats, enroute to port town of Goa. It was a base for jungle-warfare training during Burma campaign. We loved the romantic-mystique of this way-out wooded colonial-cantonment sprinkled with granite barracks and rash of ramshackle wartime hutments! I was now the highest ranking Army officer in the State of Karnataka - but even the local Station Commander was indifferent as he came under the static chain of command viz Sub-Area and Area HQ, as distinct from the command structure of the field formations or Training Establishments.

Cdr ready to rappel down a cliff-edge

JL Wing was responsible for running a series of leadership courses for the Infantry e.g. the Young Officers(YOs) course, Platoon Commander's and Commando courses as also Short Staff Course (SSC) for Capts and Weapons Instructors courses for all Arms and Services. At one end, we were just one-scale above IMA training and at the other (the SSC) it was a scaled-down Staff College course. I had personal experience of both, plus a Ranger-Commando tab- so it was full-steam ahead for me from day one.

Confidence Jump (32 feet) after a 'death' walk as a part of Cdo Trg

Almost all Instructors were 'known-devils' out of my former trainees at IMA, Cdo wing or DSSC. I could still lead by example and made it a point of demonstrating that, for effect! In all respects this was a perfect-fit i.e. tailor-made job for value addition and job satisfaction. I shall skip details so as not to be seen as 'trumpeting' my own achievements!

Both higher Headquarters were located many a hundred-mile away i.e. Command HQ at Pune and Infantry School at Mhow- which was the icing on the cake, for freedom of command!

Despina relished being the busy queen-bee amongst a horde of young Army wives. Many of them needed 'breaking-in' into Army culture being newly-weds. Many of them have now become first-ladies of higher commands-including Corps and Army Commander. They all fondly recall the learning-experience of Belgaum days! In the absence of external social distractions, all families happily engaged in welfare-activities and in-house socialising resulting in 'bonding' into a cohesive fraternity!

Athena took up a teaching job to keep herself occupied; till she met her 'knight in shining armour' in the form of a young Marine Engineer, Sanford D'Souza. He was then sailing with a Norwegian Shipping line and was on home-vacation. They had seen each other during a Sunday mass. The 'new girl' in town attracted his attention and he stalked her on a bike during walk back to Flagstaff House. The name-board Maj Gen Sharma added intrigue to the 'exotic'! Thereafter they needed little help to get introduced and to know each other better.

The Greek instincts of the Mother made her wary 'How do you know he hasn't got a girl tucked away in every port?' Nobody did; so we had to go by instinct and spoken reputation. Before an emotional-storm could brew he was recalled for sea-time; but the 'die was cast' for a repeat of the parental-precedent!

Meanwhile Arun had reached his third year of training at the National Defence Academy, Pune. During term-break he was joined by a course-mate with plans to travel to Goa. I coerced them to be adventurous and go cycling rather than by bus. Little did they realise that most of the journey was up-hill and only the last leg dipped towards the coast. After a scorching 13 hours of pedaling the first thing they did on reaching Calangute beach was to rush into the sea for relief, only to recoil as fast. The salty sea water was not kind to their saddle burns. Much of their Goa trip was then spent drinking '*feni*' on the beach and ogling at girls. Arun did venture into the sea to snoop into the nearest nudists' beach and got stranded atop a lone rock - a streak of madness is a family trait!

Concurrently, excitement erupted on the professional front. Some Young Officers went berserk in town due to perceived slights by civilians! Such robust behaviour had become a 'pattern' in recent years- all YOs were labeled 'rowdy commandos' by the locals! Some macho YOs would get carried away and get impulsively involved in such incidents.

Then the whole course would close-ranks and clam-up in the name of course or Academy spirit. Since responsibility could not be pin-pointed they would get away with warnings, to which they had become inured! It was expedient to rationalise this as hot-headed, youthful aggression and let it pass-but I had a different take. Such insidious trends undermine military discipline and erode traditional 'Officer and Gentleman' ethos.

After a particularly nasty incident involving injuries and damaged scooters, the whole course was marshaled in the Mess and the Block was cordoned off. The course was declared as suspended. It was declared that they shall remain quarantined till names of ring leaders were 'coughed-up'. As an incentive I promised that the defaulters' list shall remain 'in confidence' with me and will not be used for retributive action. It left them with two stark options- trust me or face consequences, within 24 hours! The YO Wing Commander was directed to put a round the clock guard and ensure provision of food, water and essential needs, in situ.

By next day I had the list, along with appeals for leniency! Perhaps, my 'draconian reputation' from the IMA had preceded me! I reassured them of justice and let the course resume. Meanwhile, media had sensationalised the incident and carried gory accounts to Delhi, Mhow and Pune (for discipline I was under Command HQ). The Command staff was ready to order a Staff court of Inquiry till assured that the situation was under control and within my powers.

A few days later I was directed to meet the Army Cdr, Lt Gen Ranjit Singh Dayal, MVC, who conveniently transited via a nearby Air Force base. I briefed him about the case. He nodded approval and made a deeply perceptive observation 'Why don't Young Officers of today trust their Elders, as we did? We got into bigger troubles but owned-up to our seniors'. This could only come from a hard-boiled combat commander, as 'trust' is the core-value of good soldiering! I pulled out the list from my pocket and responded 'Sir, they still do but need some coaxing! In this case I have given them my word which I would like to redeem, with your approval. Your Staff insist that I must reveal these names, but I want to deal with them in my way. I have the disciplinary powers to meet the ends of justice'. He promptly gave his approval.

That empowered me to deal with the defaulters expeditiously without compromising on demands of military discipline. Much later, a hangover of this case re-surfaced when I was the GOC-in-C. Some Commanding Officers had taken the 'adverse-remark' in the YOs course-report seriously and reflected it as a weakness in the Annual Confidential Report. The officer was due for promotion and apprehended that the 'blot' would seal his prospects. He appealed for reconsideration and redress. I expunged the offending remarks as it had served its purpose and the officer had kept his slate clean since the 'original sin'! The net gain was that the YOs never gave collective trouble in Belgaum after this incident for many years - much to the relief of the civil population and my staff! The fallout from this experience gave a positive impetus in establishing harmonious civil-military relations - a force-multiplier for a military commander!

As a result of direct liaison with the Air Force Training Command we were able to dovetail their helicopter training sorties with our Commando exercises- this was not feasible at Mhow. We tried to establish similar tie-ups with the Navy at Goa. Suddenly I was asked to forward plans for move back of the Wing to Mhow. I considered it a regressive move and reacted strongly. Their logic was that the Key Location Plan (KLP- exotic term for permanent location plans) of the Infantry School was at Mhow and all assets had been created there; hence reversion to KLP accommodation was mandatory!

I knew that the KLP for Mhow had been planned by 'innocent' Board- of- Officers (BOO) in 1960s-70s, based on available parameters. KLPs are processed at the speed of a 'paralysed centipede', whereas training-needs and environment change rapidly. The dense jungles and extensive outdoor training areas available around Mhow in the 70s had disappeared due to deforestation and creeping industrialisation. While the course capacity and content had expanded and undergone major changes. In contrast, commando training areas and facilities available at Belgaum were far more realistic.

I resisted the move plan on these grounds and that irritated higher authorities. The Staff presented doomsday scenarios (audit-objections and Parliamentary censures) to the Commandant, who rushed to see things on the ground and persuade a maverick JL Wing Commander! We had done our homework diligently and prepared elaborate presentations, including on-ground briefings. The ultimate outcome was satisfactory as a reformatted JL Wing (including Cdo training) continue to exist at Belgaum even now. I paid a minor penalty for this as the report earned then created a 'hiccup' in my next promotion- more about which later!

Meanwhile I received my orders to take over command of 7 Infantry Division deployed on the Western border. We left the Belgaum-family with a heart-full of fond memories. Many a young colt of the time have since risen to star ranks- two of them who had officiated as my Aides, are Army Commanders now. It was a well-knit and happy family and a satisfying tenure during which many close bonds were forged.

Sanford had returned from sea-time. Both families agreed and we celebrated our Daughter's engagement to him before leaving. Was this fulfillment of a 'script'- the higher purpose of our brief stay at Belgaum- who knows? Prior to move from Delhi I was offered in-situ promotion which I declined for no apparent reason! After that it was a chance meeting of the young ones and a spiral of coincidences culminating in a fateful decision which transcend human planning or logic? It was a replay of what had happened in our lifetime!

Command of the Golden Arrow Division

I took over command of the Division in 1986 from a course-mate Gen Diwan Sahni, SM. Our careers have run on parallel tracks from Academy to Army Commander; except that he was always a topper and I an incurable 'also ran'! This must be nature's way of validating a modified 'tortoise' tale. Diwan is also a fellow Muzaffarabadi from his maternal side!

7 Infantry Division has the distinction of being the most compact formation with all its Units in one station. It is also located close to its battle-stations, but is within hostile artillery range! The Division was then operationally responsible for the largest sector of the plains Border. At the time it was also deployed in interception role to check trans-border movement in the wake of the 1984 flush-out operation in Golden Temple; and as back-up to anti extremist operations by Punjab Police in the hinterland.

Addressing All Ranks of my Division

Command of a Division is a unique experience as it is the first level at which one has a balanced mix of all combat components viz. Brigades of Infantry and Artillery and Regiments of Armour, Engineers and Signals;

and Battalions of Services units (for administrative support) and ancillary units. It is a full-fledged orchestra of war. It was a dream-opportunity to indulge in a professional's passion viz to prepare my command for war, for its allotted operational task.

It was thus natural that I 'bucked like a bronco' when I was informed that I was likely to be detailed for a special task. It was to head a Ministry of Defence (MOD) Study Group to review the Military and Sainik School systems so as to optimise officers' intake from these feeder institutions. Eminent academics, from public and private sector institutions, were to be co-opted as members. In my view this was a travesty of all logic and commonsense- a high-school pass Infantry officer, on proving-trials for higher command, to head such a study was a cruel joke? Despite my refusal, pleading and lobbying I could only secure a deferment, which was providential as an operational emergency intervened abruptly.

At Firing Ranges with Comdr & Staff Arty
Bde for Live firing Practice Camps

After dealing with that exigency, I did complete the MoD assignment during the latter part of my tenure. For this I had to travel frequently to Delhi and also visit many Schools to get a first hand feel of the problem. It culminated in presentations to the Minister of Defence. All our recommendations were well received and approved. It was particularly satisfying to be profusely complimented by many Principals and teachers!

I found interaction with the academics a highly stimulating experience. But let me revert to my main job.

As mentioned earlier, my command was so compact that I could blow a 'whistle' and collect all my Unit commanders or visit any sub-unit on training within 30 minutes. But the flip-side was that any Havildar (Sergeant) Major could also blow his whistle and pull-out manpower from training for administrative demands; thus disrupting continuity and integrity of training.

As GOC I would be mad to interfere with Unit or sub-unit level training. My role was to lay down training policy that works on the ground and let the system run on auto-mode! But for that I had to know the grassroots-gaps between paper policies and ground-realities. The formal feedback system of training reports, visits and conferences do not always reflect reality. My location enabled me to employ innovative ways to do a reality-check and evolve creative solutions. One such was an Intensive Training Cycle (ITC) for one sub-unit at a time to camp outside Sergeant-Major's whistle range, while leaving adequate strength for security and administrative duties, leave, courses etc. Some of these innovations have since become standard practice and are still surviving.

It is normal to review operational plans especially at the start of a command-tenure. In this process grey areas emerged in relation to my riverine sector and employment of Corps reserves in my sector. I shared these with the Corps Commander, Lt Gen Tubby Nayar-my former boss from Manipur days. But it is not easy to unfreeze mindsets or existing plans in the first go!

A two-sided uncontrolled map exercise was organised to war-game all scenarios. That did cause a significant thaw. But the clincher came when a threat of real war developed as a sequel to Exercise BRASSTACKS- a live exercise by our Strike Corps south of my Sector. Our opponents across the Border felt threatened, mobilised their Army and moved their Strategic Reserves- one was within striking range of my low- threat sector.

Indian Army reacted with full scale mobilisation. War plans were suitably adapted- more in line with some of my suggestions- and operationalised. Thereafter everyone remained in trigger-finger readiness for months, in dug-outs and underground bunkers with live mines strewn all along the front. This was as close as anyone can get to a full-scale shooting war.

A few words on the context of this 'Un-fought war' of Rajiv Gandhi (PM)-Arun Singh (Def Minister)- Gen Sundarji (Army Chief) era. Our flamboyant Chief had planned a major mechanised forces exercise close to the western border. All units were carrying full scales of live ammunition; that is not a training norm. Military adversaries are highly sensitive to new capabilities that enable change in 'intentions and plans'. This was bound to trigger a spiral of mistrust, mobilisation and all else mentioned above.

The US satellites had picked this up and our PM was asked awkward questions. Recently it has come to light that Dr Raja Ramanna, head of India's Atomic Energy Commission, who was then in Vienna was invited for dinner by Dr AQ Khan of Pakistan. During that the latter categorically declared that 'If India tries to attack Pak nuclear plants, we will blow up Bhabha Atomic Research Centre (BARC) in no time'. This was passed on to the PM; who was reportedly not in the loop? And thus Op TRIDENT remained an 'un-fought war' by a whisker. But it had kept us on 'roast' in the oven for months! War plans were validated and fine-tuned, as in the case of my Southern sector, but tactical surprise was compromised due to visible preparations. These had to be reworked. A small compensation was that reports (ACR) of this period were given same weightage as Battle Reports.

To be kept waiting in starting-blocks at peak war-readiness is stressful-far more than actual fighting. In this state, two Capts who were carrying out border familiarisation along the Southern sector strayed across the Border. The navigation blunder hit them when they ran into a Pak Rangers Post. Both sides were surprised but defenders recovered first and grabbed the 'prize-catch' of a jeep with two officers, maps etc! Radio-silence was in force so we only found out about the 'lost-sheep' after last-light. Then all hell broke loose and 'hotlines' started crackling at all levels to ascertain their survival/status!

The newly posted Capt had brought his new bride to Station. This raw girl from a South-Indian state only knew vernacular and a few words of English. Most families from North Indian States had moved back to safer places and those staying back were being put through paces of civil-defence preparations in event of a shooting war. Despina had experienced war earlier, including air-raids and shelling, during Arab-Israeli war of 1956 in Suez Canal zone. She was able to comfort the families and keep the home-front organised. She took the distraught new bride under her wings and moved her into the Flagstaff House- where shelters and trenches were being dug!

The day after the incident Command HQ informed that the Army Cdr had taken off by helicopter to visit the concerned Bde - he had commanded it once. From my Tactical HQ, travel time by road was the same as his flying time. I barely managed to reach a few minutes before him. When I informed the Corps Cdr, he asked 'What for?' and I replied 'You tell me?' That said it all, between us! The Bde Cdr briefed the Army Cdr as best as he knew. Thereafter all further questions were met with a stoic silence - we knew nothing more! But he left us in no doubt that such a lapse would not have occurred in his time- we nodded obediently!

I was surprised when some fertile 'intelligence' heads in Delhi conjectured whether this was one of my trans-border missions gone awry? One had done 'nutty' things in counter insurgency but in a war-situation covered by Geneva conventions- no way! This was imagination gone wild even by Intelligence standards; or was it a reflection of my 'image' in their book, I wondered?

After many days the 'prisoners' were repatriated after they had been fully 'squeezed' by interrogators. They were debriefed by our experts and a formal court of inquiry was held. Nothing incriminating was found with regard to their conduct during captivity or interrogation. It had been a careless but accidental lapse. It was my belief that no one should be crucified for an innocent lapse of judgment. I recommended summary disposal of the case at my level rather than a court martial, as *was favoured at Command level.*

My Corps Cdr backed me so I was allowed to have my way. Both officers were summarily awarded punishments- loss of service and severe-reprimand; but retained in service. But this time I had been fooled- their story of having torn up and flushed/swallowed identity documents was a fabrication as the Cards came back from across the Border after some time. Our adversaries had retained them as leverage to blackmail and 'turn' these officers into informers? But they failed- did the change of heart of my officers happen due to humane-handling or some other reason is a matter of speculation! But I had learnt a lesson 'Beware! When you trust, you will win some and lose some'. But 'trust' is still worth it!

Family Group - Post Wedding Picture

Meanwhile Athena's wedding date was arranged by mutual convenience- it was 15 Aug, to coincide with our date (also Despina's Name's Day- auspicious by Greek Orthodox tradition). I was sanctioned a week's leave, as the operational situation was still hot. We chose to celebrate the occasion at Belgaum in view of the disturbed conditions in Border States. In the finest tradition of the Army my successor at JL Wing extended all possible help. My old colleagues contributed generously of time and energy and attended all functions in strength, to make this family event memorable. Such camaraderie is what makes the Army a cohesive family.

Arun, who was in his final term in IMA, could get away very briefly. My eldest Cousin RL, Sister and Brother in law, two younger Brothers and Bhabhis came with their children; as did some close friends from far and wide including the Schrags. We had decided to keep the celebrations solemn and simple. Later the young couple went up North to seek blessings of family Elders and spend some time with us before hitting the high seas to sail together into a new life. That day I was awarded the Chief's Commendation citation for distinguished contribution during my tenure in Army Headquarters- it sure was a lucky day!

Family Group from Jammu

By the time I rejoined, full scale de-induction was in progress. This can be as hazardous as the launch phase, especially de-mining and defusing of live explosives and ammunition. We then reverted to an even keel of peacetime soldiering. But there were many lessons to be learnt from Op TRIDENT especially those related to grey areas of mobilisation and management of civil affairs in areas where crops are cultivated up to the Border and up to the hour that live bullets start flying. All this must have been fully streamlined in the context of the new 'cold start' doctrine- whatever it be!

Shortly thereafter there was a change of higher command. For a second time Lt Gen VK Sood relieved Lt Gen Nayar who took over as Western Army Commander. The latter had top-rated the Golden Arrow Division's readiness status and operational responses. So the new command line-up left me in a happy place!

Another Traditional Farewell

The normal tenure for command of a Division was 18 months, subject to two command reports. As soon as I completed the criteria I was posted as Chief of Staff of 16 Corps deployed along the Line of Control in J&K. Coincidentally the other two Div Cdrs were also posted out around the same time. We were all dined out on the same day. In his farewell speech the Corps Commander gave higher precedence and time to my Division which prompted the other GsOC- both senior to me- to suggest that I respond on their behalf also! I did; but not without detecting more than a tinge of 'envy' in the gesture!

Before I left command of the Division, we were able to attend Arun's Commissioning Parade at IMA Dehra Dun. He had done better than me in all respects- he graduated much higher in 'order of merit' as an Under

Officer and earned Academy Blues in polo, riding and generally excelled in sports and extra-curricular activities. Happily for us he needed little persuasion to exercise his parental claim to be commissioned into 2nd Bn The GRENADIERS, despite a sub-conscious perception that it would be seen as wanting to grow under my wings!

I was promoted twice thereafter and handled assignments at strategic levels. But I have decided to close the present narrative at this stage for reasons briefly covered in the following Epilogue.

Epilogue

It has been a breathless- recall of memories of more than half a century (1936-88)! It is time to pause.

If it has been an unevenly exciting narrative, it is because real life is like that- never a straight line or a smooth curve. We had our highs and lows, including a reckless romance with a fairy-tale finale, a traumatic war-experience and crashing of a glass-ceiling!

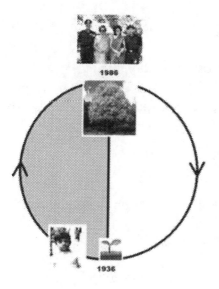

There were survival-struggles in early years of family life, a walk-through fire and a mixed bag of bumps and blessings. A rising career-trajectory and contented family-life was intersected with cross-roads in life. One wonders if it was pre-scripted or a series of ad-hoc coincidences or divine interventions. After eight decades, I do have a view on that now, but I shall reserve it for later!

Each one of you will take away a different lesson from this story, based on one's level of consciousness and values! I do hope that none will miss my testimony on two core issues---firstly, the essential inclusiveness of humanity, despite conflicting identity-labels and beliefs, as is exemplified in our case. These fracture-lines will not disappear but their toxic effects can be sublimated! Secondly, that basic human values e.g. truth, trust, love, compassion and selflessness remain relevant, even in the military. These worked for us and we were not special!

There is a purpose and continuity in this narrative. The continuity is in the growth-process from human-seeds into two full-blown persons: one a hard-core military professional and the other his mate. The imagery of a 'circle' illustrates the process. The left half - from the low-end of the circle (the seed-spot) to the top represents the growth of physical-skills, mental ability and achievements in the outside world. It is a high pressure world of competitive power, position and prestige. My narrative thus far has covered this phase.

We realised, sooner than later, that it was mostly a game of 'chasing-shadows', for fleeting gains! True happiness and contentment remain elusive as they have to be found in our inner space, within oneself. We also turned inwards to the real source of power and bliss. This shift shall be the focus of my next story.

I have therefore chosen to apply closure to the present narrative at this stage. I believe that the 'purpose of life' is to harmonise the inner and outer dimensions and connect to the 'power' within! A subtle message of this story was to build the base for that.

Reflections

Let me restate the short-point of the above in less philosophical terms.

The first 50 years of our life was spent in pursuit of personal and professional development and raising a family. These are basic survival and growth needs. One resisted the temptation to get obsessed with reports, recognition, and money/ material gains. Irresistably, the ego-balloon keeps blowing up-one had to keep deflating it- fortunately some seniors helped!

Did these bring real happiness-we did not think so? We were both well grounded.

As we entered the second part of the life-cycle issues like 'purpose and meaning of life' became important. We realised that 'satisfaction' from achievements and material things leads to virtual- happiness which fades away- it is like a mirage! Bliss lies within us- a realisation that comes later - but not to all, as they do not know how?

Tailpiece

I end my Musings with a sense of satisfaction at having kept faith with the three rules that I had set for myself:-

No fabrications or fudging;
No trumpeting, and
No malice.

Our Credo: *Vasudhaiva Kutumbkam* (all the Universe is one family); *Om Shanti* (Peace on earth and goodwill to all mankind).

Printed in the United States
By Bookmasters